Beginning Reading Practices

Beginning Reading Practices
Building Reading and Vocabulary Strategies

SILVIA   SILVA   MACIAS.

Keith S. Folse

Ann Arbor

THE UNIVERSITY OF MICHIGAN PRESS

Acknowledgments

I would like to thank the numerous professionals who gave their expert advice in the design of some of the activities used in this textbook. Among these professionals, I would especially like to acknowledge certain members of TESLMW-L (the materials writers group on the TESL-L electronic communication list) who offered suggestions: Tracy Henninger-Chiang, Martha Grace Lowe, Eileen Prince, Lynn Ramage, Judee Reel, Susie Robertshaw, David Ross, Barbara Stoops, Anthea Tillyer, and Joe McVeigh. Both TESL-L and TESLMW-L have proven time and time again to be excellent sources of new teaching ideas and techniques. In addition, I am grateful to David Grahame, Alan Juffs, and the reviewers for their invaluable suggestions and ideas.

Contents

To the Teacher   ix

Lesson 1. Exercises and Skills Practices   **1**
     Context Clues: Opposites   1
     Language Focus: Connectors *and, but, so*   4

Lesson 2. Extended Reading Fluency Practices   **22**
     Nonprose: Class Schedule   22
     Nonfiction: U.S. Map   24
     Fiction: Folktale: A Crane's Payment for a Man's Kindness   26
     News Reports: True or False?   28
     Reading/Discussion/Writing: Smoking at Work   30

Lesson 3. Exercises and Skills Practices   **33**
     Context Clues: Descriptions   33
     Language Focus: Pronouns   36

Lesson 4. Extended Reading Fluency Practices   **54**
     Nonprose: U.S. Presidents   54
     Nonfiction: Giraffes   55
     Fiction: Mini mystery: The Case of the Stolen Painting   58
     News Reports: True or False?   61
     Reading/Discussion/Writing: Cheating on a Test at School   62

Lesson 5. Exercises and Skills Practices   **65**
     Context Clues: Logical Groupings   65
     Language Focus: Markers *this, that, these, those*   69

Lesson 6. Extended Reading Fluency Practices   **90**
     Nonprose: Menu   90
     Nonfiction: Is Eating Fish Really Healthy?   91
     Fiction: Folktale: The Woodcutter and His Axe   95
     News Reports: True or False?   99
     Reading/Discussion/Writing: Tipping   100

Lesson 7. Reading Tasks and Vocabulary Activities   **103**
    Reading Tasks   103
    Crossword Puzzle 1   111
    Vocabulary Tasks   112
    Crossword Puzzle 2   117

Lesson 8. Short Story: The Lady or the Tiger?   **119**

Reading Rate Charts   **127**
    Timed Word Selection Rate Chart   128
    Timed Reading Rate Chart   128

Answer Key   **129**

Individual Vocabulary Notebook   **133**

To the Teacher

This book contains exercises that provide practice in basic reading skills for beginning students of English as a second language (ESL). It is intended for an intensive course of approximately eight to ten weeks in which at least one hour per day is devoted to reading improvement.

This text has six main goals:
1. to develop students' vocabulary (since lack of vocabulary is a severe handicap at this level);
2. to teach students skills that will help them deal with unfamiliar vocabulary (such as context clues practices);
3. to teach important reading skills at a beginning level;
4. to help students develop and use these skills through gradual, sequential practices (ranging from single sentences to real, longer reading selections);
5. to give students reading passages at the appropriate language level (i.e., passages written at a beginning level that therefore do not overwhelm students) in which they can apply their new reading skills; and
6. to develop students' awareness and use of important strategies so that students can improve their reading ability and learn to become independent readers in English.

The reading skills emphasized in this text include using context clues, drawing conclusions, understanding factual information, finding the main idea, reading for specific information, sequencing material, making predictions, using outlines to understand text organization, summarizing material, raising students' awareness of the role of a linguistic point within a passage, and reading for enjoyment.

This text consists of eight lessons. Lessons 1 through 6 should be covered in pairs (e.g., 1–2, 3–4, 5–6). The odd-numbered lessons are skills practices while the even-numbered lessons offer real reading practices. Lesson 7 and lesson 8 are independent; each follows a different format. Lesson 7 offers a variety of fun vocabulary exercises that can be done at any point during the course. On the other hand, lesson 8, which consists of the short story "The Lady or the Tiger?" is more challenging and should therefore be done near the end of the course.

It is important to note that many of the problems used in the exercises in the odd-numbered lessons (i.e., 1, 3, 5) are actual sentences taken either from reading passages in the same lesson or from the reading selections found in the complementing even-numbered lesson (i.e., 2, 4, 6).

Contents of Lessons 1, 3, 5 (skills practices)

Context Clues
    Exercises 1, 2, 3

different kinds of general contexts that practice words that students will find in the readings

Language Focus
    Exercises 4, 5

various linguistic features that are important to understanding the organization of a passage

Sentence Study
    Exercises 6, 7

answering specific information or drawing conclusions from a single sentence

Main Idea
    Exercises 8, 9

the main idea of a paragraph

Scanning
    Exercise 10

scanning for specific information

Sequencing/Prediction
    Exercise 11

analyzing the sequence of material and predicting what might come next

Following Directions
    Exercise 12

following directions to complete a simple task

Faster Reading
    Exercises 13, 15, 17, 19, 21
    Exercises 14, 16, 18, 20, 22

improving reading rate: word practices,
timed reading practices

Vocabulary Recall
    Exercise 23

multiple-choice questions for rapid review

Contents of Lessons 2, 4, 6 (reading selections)

Nonprose
Exercise 1

nonprose selections that include a class schedule, a listing of U.S. presidents, and a menu

Nonfiction
Exercise 2

nonfiction selections that feature prereading, reading, and outlining exercises

Fiction
Exercise 3

fiction selections that feature reading selections, interactive reading questions within the selection, and summary writing

News Reports: True or False?
Exercise 4

brief news reports that students read and determine whether or not the reports are true

Reading/Discussion/Writing
Exercise 5

an "advice" letter followed by four response letters that deals with a contemporary topic; this exercise practices reading, discussion, and writing

This text was written especially for beginning-level students. Obviously the vocabulary employed has been controlled to match the students' English ability. In addition, the grammatical structures used in the exercises and selections have been controlled to coordinate them with those most likely being studied in any beginning ESL grammar or integrated skills class. Thus, the exercises in this text provide not only indispensable practice of vocabulary and reading skills but also further reinforcement of the grammatical structures being emphasized at this level.

Since the reading level and grammatical structures in each lesson gradually increase in difficulty, the lessons for the most part should be done in numerical order whenever possible. This is especially true for the timed reading exercises, which gradually increase in length as well as in difficulty. An exception to this rule is lesson 7. The exercises in lesson 7 may be done at any time during the course. They are designed to provide a break from the other more information-laden lessons. Lesson 8 is perhaps the most challenging lesson and should be attempted after the students have completed most of the material in the other lessons.

The progress charts found after lesson 8 are for the timed word and timed reading exercises. Students should be encouraged to record their progress, as this will help them see their improvement. The instructions for completing these charts can be found on page 127.

There is an Answer Key for most of the exercises in this text. These answers are provided so that students will use the Answer Key after they have actually done the exercises. It is further hoped that students will use the Answer Key to detect their mistakes and then return to the exercise to discover the source of their error. The Answer Key also makes it possible for students engaged in independent study to use this workbook. (Some teachers do not wish their students to have the Answer Key. Since the key is only a few pages long, it is quite easy to remove the pages with the aid of a ruler, staple the pages together, and keep them until the end of the term. In fact, this can be done by the students themselves on the first day of the class.)

Following the Answer Key are several pages on which students may write down new vocabulary words as they are encountered. There is enough space so that the students may write not only the word but also a definition and example if they want to do this. Students should be encouraged to use this part of the text, as they will certainly find many new vocabulary items within this text as well as their other books. Vocabulary enrichment is a vital skill for students at the beginning level.

Throughout the book are twenty reading strategies. These strategies are not connected to any one lesson or part of a lesson. In fact, they are not in any set order and can be covered in any sequence that the instructor deems appropriate. Research has shown the value of raising students' awareness of learning strategies; the benefits to second language learners can be enormous. Though these strategies can be taught in various ways, it is recommended that the instructor present the strategy and then have students discuss whether they think this strategy will be beneficial to their learning and how the strategy can be directly applied to their learning situation.

Using the Exercises in Lessons 1, 3, 5 (skills practice exercises)

Context Clues

Exercises 1–3 provide practice in using context clues to help determine the meaning of an unfamiliar word. This ability is invaluable to the student of English as a second language. The vocabulary practiced in these exercises is actual vocabulary from reading selections in this lesson or the next.

Exercise 1. In this exercise, students practice using context clues to solve the meaning of a key word. Students must read a sentence and then complete it with any word that is logical based on the context provided. Several answers may be possible; teachers should go over this exercise in class to check students' answers. When they have completed this exercise, students should work in pairs or small groups to discuss their answers. Then they may turn to the end of the lesson to find a listing of possible answers as well as explanations of the sentences. Each of the three lessons focuses on a different kind of context clue. (Lesson 1 focuses on opposites, lesson 3 on descriptions, and lesson 5 on logical groupings.)

Exercise 2. This exercise consists of sentences that contain an italicized term. After each problem, there are three possible meanings given. Students will read the problem and then use their knowledge of context clues to determine which of the three given meanings is correct.

Exercise 3. This exercise also consists of sentences that contain an italicized term. After each problem, there are two spaces provided. In the first blank, students should analyze the context and then write down their best guess of the meaning of the term. Next, the students should consult a dictionary for the precise meaning of the word, and in the second blank, they should write down this meaning.

Language Focus

Exercises 4–5 help students to see how certain linguistic or rhetorical points are used to organize English prose. These exercises help students to anticipate what is coming next in a sentence as well as in a paragraph. Each of these lessons focuses on a different linguistic feature. Lesson 1 focuses on connectors (*and, but, so),* lesson 3 on pronouns, and lesson 5 on the markers *this, that, these, those.*

Exercise 4. In this exercise, students are to demonstrate their passive awareness of certain linguistic or rhetorical features.

Exercise 5. This exercise is similar to the previous exercise but demands a higher cognitive level of performance.

Sentence Study

Understanding a given sentence is often the key to understanding an entire paragraph. For this reason, sentence study (exercises 6 and 7) is an important reading skill to master, especially at the lower levels.

Exercise 6. In this exercise, students read a sentence and then demonstrate how well they have grasped the details by answering a question about the sentence. The format is multiple-choice (A, B, C, or D).

Exercise 7. In this exercise, students indicate how well they can understand a given sentence and form a logical conclusion about it. Students read a statement and four conclusions. They must indicate which of the four conclusions is correct based on the information contained in the original sentence.

Finding the Main Idea

Being able to read a new piece of reading material and determine not only the general topic but also the writer's main idea is a critical skill for all readers. Exercises 8–9 provide pertinent practice in this skill.

Exercise 8. Students are to read a paragraph rapidly to determine its main idea. This exercise also follows a multiple-choice format.

Exercise 9. In this exercise, students are to read a paragraph, find the one unrelated sentence, and cross through it to delete it. Then, students are to read the four possible main ideas that follow each paragraph and choose the best answer.

Scanning

In exercise 10, students will practice scanning for specific information. Before each paragraph, there are two multiple-choice questions that test the students' understanding of details. This exercise helps develop reading comprehension while encouraging improvement of reading rate.

Sequencing/Prediction

In exercise 11, there are four paragraphs that have usually been taken from latter portions of this lesson and the next. Each paragraph has been split into three parts, and each part has been put into one of three columns. In column A, there are four initial paragraph parts. In column B, there are four middle paragraph parts. In column C, there are four concluding paragraph parts. Students are to draw lines to connect the three parts of each paragraph. This exercise practices logical sequencing of material as well as prediction of what kind of material should follow a certain sentence or word. It also offers further vocabulary practice and reinforcement.

Following Directions

In exercise 12, students will read directions to complete a simple task. Students are to follow the directions exactly so that all students come up with a similar final product.

Improving Reading Speed

After general reading comprehension, perhaps the most serious problem encountered by ESL students is reading speed or reading rate. This might be true for a variety of reasons. It could be due to the students' lack of vocabulary knowledge at this level. Practice with context clues (exercises 1–3) will help to overcome this. This problem might also be due to a limited knowledge of grammatical structures. In order to read well, ESL students need a solid grasp of basic English syntax, that is, a good grammar base. On the other hand, this reading rate deficiency could also be due to the fact that the students' native language is not read from left to right as English is, or it may be due in part to the fact that the students' alphabet uses letters or characters that are very different from those in the English alphabet. The timed word selections (13, 15, 17, 19, 21) will work on these two problems. Finally, the timed reading exercises (14, 16, 18, 20, 22) allow students the opportunity to test all their reading skills, including reading rate, since each of these last exercises is timed.

Timed Word Selection Exercises

In exercises 13, 15, 17, 19, and 21, students must read a word and then find the same word in a group of five words that look similar. For example, the students must circle the word *once* in the following example:

once | one   only   other   old   once

The goals of these exercises are to train students' eye movements in a left-to-right pattern and to provide practice in recognition of similarly shaped letters and letter combinations.

To improve reading speed, these exercises should be timed, thus encouraging students to work as rapidly as possible. It is recommended that teachers give students thirty seconds to complete the twenty-five problems in these exercises. Students should then correct their answers. Since it is difficult for students to catch their own errors in this kind of "proofreading" exercise, it is recommended that students exchange books and check each other's work to ensure accurate correcting. For each incorrect answer, students lose one correct answer. This penalty will encourage students to work carefully as well as rapidly. Afterward, students should record the number of correct answers on the progress chart at the end of this text (p. 128).

Timed Reading Exercises

Each of exercises 14, 16, 18, 20, and 22 consists of a short reading selection (usually two to four paragraphs) followed by five multiple-choice questions. Students have *four** minutes to read the selection *and* answer the questions. Students may look back in the selection for answers if necessary. However, the teacher should point out that this is a time-consuming process, and after not finishing this exercise once or twice, students will realize the importance of reading the selection carefully the first time. There is no penalty for incorrect answers, thus the score is the number of correct answers. Students should record their scores on the chart at the back of the text (p. 128). Though this is primarily designed as a test of an individual's silent reading ability, oral reading skills may be practiced by having students read parts of the selection aloud after time has been called and all answers have been checked.

The questions have three possible answers (A, B, or C). Because choice C is sometimes "both A and B," students are encouraged to read all the answers very carefully before making their final choice. These timed reading exercises require students to use the skills that they have been practicing in the other exercises, for example, understanding details, forming conclusions, and using context clues. Whenever possible, each of the five questions emphasizes a different reading skill. Teachers should use the following chart in counseling students concerning their reading improvement:

Question 1. Main idea of a paragraph (See exercises 8–9.)
Question 2. Context clues (See exercises 1–3.)
Question 3. Conclusions (See exercise 7.)
Question 4. Information (Details) (See exercises 6 and 10.)
Question 5. Information (Details) (See exercises 6 and 10.)

Before attempting to do a timed reading exercise, it is highly recommended that teachers do some type of prereading activity in order to increase student interest in the reading selection as well as develop the students' anticipation skills. The acquisition and subsequent development of good anticipation skills is a key factor in reading proficiency. The value of such skills, especially to ESL students, should not be underestimated.

For example, if the reading is about a country, the teacher should write the name of the country on the board and ask the students if they know its location, people, language, weather, etc. The instructor should also ask the students to come up with a list of vocabulary words (or concepts) that they expect to find in the selection. For example, in reading about a nation, many students will come up with concept of border, but very few will actually know the term at this level. In addition, they will probably not know the word *lie*

---

* Four minutes is merely a suggested time limit. It is a time restriction that has worked well with beginning ESL students who have used this text. The actual time limit used can be increased or decreased to fit the average or above-average student in a given class. It should be noted that the timed readings gradually increase in individual sentence length, overall length, lexical difficulty, and syntactical difficulty. Therefore, it is highly recommended that instructors select one timed reading rate to be used throughout the entire text. Since it is supposed that students' reading skills will improve as the timed reading exercises become more difficult, students should have little difficulty working within the given time restrictions of these exercises.

(meaning "to occupy a place") at this point either. Teachers may elect to tell their students these words outright or help them to learn to anticipate such words through this previewing activity and then let them guess the meaning through context by themselves.

A Note about the Timed Word Selection and Timed Reading Exercises

In general, the exercises in each lesson should be done in the same order in which they have already been sequenced. Vocabulary has been recycled within the timed reading exercises, and doing these out of sequence might mean that a student would find an unfamiliar word that was actually introduced in a richer context in an earlier exercise. However, instructors may wish to digress somewhat when doing these timed word and timed reading exercises. If teachers follow the existing numerical order (i.e., 13, 14, 15, 16, etc.), they will do these two types of exercises alternately. However, an equally valid method (and somewhat easier according to some teachers) involves having students do all of the timed word selection exercises first and then do all of the timed reading exercises (i.e., 13, 15, 17, 19, and 21; then 14, 16, 18, 20, and 22). The preference lies with the individual instructor, the students, and the teaching situation. Regardless of the sequence ultimately chosen as more appropriate, teachers should make every effort to see that students do not look ahead at any timed exercises since this will of course adversely affect their reading rate results.

Vocabulary Recall

Rapid word recognition and the acquisition of a good, solid vocabulary are fundamental to learning how to read effectively. Exercise 23 tests vocabulary recall. Teachers may choose to have students do this in class, as homework, or as a test. This exercise reviews material that has been presented within the given lesson. It has a multiple-choice format.

Using the Exercises in Lessons 2, 4, 6 (reading selections)

Nonprose

In exercise 1, students will read information in a nonprose format. This exercise will provide practice in reading a class schedule (lesson 2), a listing of U.S. presidents (lesson 4), and a menu (lesson 6). These exercises consist of the nonprose reading selection followed by a series of questions.

Nonfiction

In exercise 2, students will read nonfiction passages. These include passages on U.S. geography (lesson 2), giraffes (lesson 4), and food and health (lesson 6). This exercise has three parts. Part 1 is a prereading activity. Part 2 is the actual reading selection. Part 3 is an outlining activity that is designed to focus students' attention on the organizational patterns found in the reading selections.

Fiction

In this exercise, students will read three fiction selections. These include a Japanese folktale (lesson 2), a minimystery (lesson 4), and a Thai folktale (lesson 6). Rather than the typical set of comprehension questions found at the end of a reading selection, these selections have both comprehension and prediction questions *within the selections*. The purpose of this format of interactive questions is to stimulate a constant stream of questions about the material in the reader's mind. This format is actually much closer to what good readers do and therefore better represents the *teaching* of reading versus the typical *testing* of reading. This exercise is followed by a directed discussion activity and a brief guided summary writing activity.

News Reports: True or False?

Exercise 4 consists of three short news reports. Though all three of the reports look real, only one of the three is real. Students are to read the three reports, choose which one they think is true, and write a defense of their choice by explaining in writing the reasons for their answer. The main goal of this exercise is reading fluency, i.e., volume or amount of reading. Students read the three news items, guess which one is really true, and then re-read them to verify this initial guess.

Reading/Discussion/Writing

Exercise 5 consists of a "Dear Advisor" type of letter in which someone has written with a problem in hopes of getting good advice and possible solutions to the person's problems. Following the original writer's letter are four possible reply letters all offering very different kinds of advice.

The exercise consists of four parts. In part one of this exercise, students are to read the original letter. In part two, students are to work in pairs or small groups to discuss their answers to the comprehension and expansion questions. In part three, students must read the four reply letters and decide which letter has the best advice and which has the worst advice. In part four, students will write their own original responses to offer advice concerning the problem at hand.

Using the Exercises in Lesson 7 (reading and vocabulary tasks)

Lesson 7 consists of three different kinds of exercises: reading tasks, crossword puzzles, and vocabulary building tasks. The four reading tasks require students to read information and then use this information to complete a task. The crossword puzzles work on not only vocabulary but also skimming and scanning (e.g., number 6 down is a topic of a reading on p. 107). Finally, the vocabulary building exercises are fun word association activities.

The exercises in this lesson can be done at any time during the course. They should be done when other readings are too long or too heavy and a break from the regular routine is desired. In addition, these exercises may be done in any sequence.

Using the Exercises in Lesson 8 (short story)

Lesson 8 consists of a single short story (approximately 2,300 words long). There is a preliminary vocabulary exercise that should be done before students attempt this story. The rest of the lesson consists of the short story followed by reading comprehension and discussion questions.

Lesson 1

Exercises and Skills Practices

Exercise 1. Context Clues: Opposites

Complete each sentence with your own words. Then discuss your answers with a partner or with your class. There may be no single best answer at times. Possible answers are on page 21.

1. Peter is tall, but his brother is ___short___ .

2. The house on the left is small, but the house on the right is ___big/large___

3. A box is square, but a circle is ___round___ .

4. This movie is new, but that movie is ___old___ .

5. Many people in that country are poor, but some people are ___rich___ .

6. My pencil is very thick, but your pencil is very ___thin___ .

7. This picture is only black, white, and gray, but that picture is very ___colorful___ .

8. Not many people know this book, but that book is very ___popular/famous___ .

9. His house is to the east, but her house is to the ___west___ .

10. This class is difficult, but English class is ___easy___ .

11. Your answer is wrong, but my answer is ___correct/right___

12. Some countries have a queen, but other countries have a ___king___ .

13. These two coins are different, but these two coins are the ___same___ .

14. These apples smell good, but these old shoes smell ___bad___ !

15. She likes English class very much, but she ___doesn't like / hates___ math class.

1

Exercise 2. Context Clues

In each of these sentences, you will find an italicized word or group of words. Read the three choices and then decide which choice means about the same as the italicized word or words. Circle the letter of your answer.

1. How can I *find out* Peter's telephone number? Is there a list of telephone numbers?
    A. make
    B. tell
    C. learn

2. No one really *thinks* that the U.S. government will change the system in the near future.
    A. believes
    B. understands
    C. wants

3. Georgia became an English colony in 1733 when General James Oglethorpe arrived there to *set up* the city of Savannah, which is located on the Atlantic Ocean.
    A. begin
    B. choose
    C. talk about

4. I'm *concerned* about your health. You smoke too much and you don't eat good food.
    A. happy
    B. worried
    C. asking

5. The *population* of that city is about 3,000,000.
    A. size of the state
    B. cost of a house
    C. number of people

6. He became almost totally *deaf.* In fact, he could only hear his last great works in his imagination because he could not hear at all.
    A. not able to think
    B. not able to like
    C. not able to hear

Exercise 3. Context Clues + Dictionary Work

In each of these sentences, you will find an italicized word or group of words. Read the sentence and then write your guess about the meaning of the word. Then look up the word in a dictionary and write the real meaning.

1. The bird was hurt, so he put some medicine on the bird's *injury* to make it better.

    YOUR GUESS: _____

    REAL MEANING: _physical harm_

2. *In the wild*, flamingos live for fifteen to twenty years. (In captivity, they live longer.)

    YOUR GUESS: *Jungle*

    REAL MEANING: *Natural state (habitat) / jungle*

3. (In the wild, flamingos live for fifteen to twenty years.) *In captivity*, they live longer.

    YOUR GUESS: _____

    REAL MEANING: *Confinement*

4. At age five, Beethoven studied the violin, and he soon started with other musical *instruments*.

    YOUR GUESS: _____

    REAL MEANING: *device producing musical sound*

5. Ohyo asked his wife to make some more cloth. At first, she was *reluctant* to do this. Then Ohyo talked to her about this for a long time. "Please, please, please make some more cloth for me," he asked. Finally she agreed to do this for him.

    YOUR GUESS: _____

    REAL MEANING: *unwilling*

6. I studied Chinese a long, long time ago, but I can *still* remember some words.

    YOUR GUESS: _____

    REAL MEANING: *up to now*

7. For some people, it is easy to *compose* a song. However, I am sure that I could never write a song.

    YOUR GUESS: _____

    REAL MEANING: *to create/write*

8. The American movie *industry* makes hundreds of movies every year.

    YOUR GUESS: _____

    REAL MEANING: *productions*

9. Flamingos *reproduce* once a year. The female lays one egg, and for thirty days the parents take turns sitting on the egg.

    YOUR GUESS: _____

Flamingo
USA 29

    REAL MEANING: *to produce offspring.*

10. Beethoven was born in Germany and grew up there. However, in 1792, he moved to Vienna, Austria. Beethoven spent the *rest* of his life in Austria.

    YOUR GUESS: _____

    REAL MEANING: *remainder.*

11. This book is not mine. *Perhaps* it is Brenda's book. Let's ask her.

    YOUR GUESS: _____

    REAL MEANING: *Maybe*

12. This paper is very, very *important*. Keep it in your desk. Be very careful with it. Do not lose it.

    YOUR GUESS: _____

    REAL MEANING: *Valuable*

13. Many *farmers* in that state grow corn and wheat.

    YOUR GUESS: _____

    REAL MEANING: *a person who operates a farm.*

14. California has many people. *In fact,* California is now the biggest state in population.

    YOUR GUESS: _____

    REAL MEANING: *someting that is true.*

Exercise 4. Language Focus: Connectors *and, but, so*

Each paragraph has one connector. Read the paragraph and then choose which of the two connectors is correct. Circle the correct connector.

1. Flamingos live in colonies or groups. The female lays one egg, [so, <u>and</u>] for thirty days the parents take turns sitting on the egg. In the wild, flamingos live for fifteen to twenty years. In captivity, they live longer.

2. William Faulkner was a famous writer. Faulkner lived most of his life in Oxford, Mississippi. He traveled a little, [<u>but</u>, so] even after he became famous, he still preferred to stay in the small town of Oxford.

3. Beethoven's full name was Ludwig van Beethoven. He was born in Bonn, Germany, in 1770. At age five, Beethoven studied the violin, [and, so] he soon started with other musical instruments. When he was only twelve, he got his first job as an organ player. He wrote four musical compositions that year.

4. The man saw a bird. The bird was hurt. It was a bad injury, [but, so] the man put some medicine on the bird's injury to make it better.

Exercise 5. Language Focus: Connectors *and, but, so*

Each of the sentences has a blank. Complete the sentence by writing *and, but,* or *so* on the line. Sometimes more than one answer is possible.

1. I'm tired, _____but_____ I'm going to play tennis with Joe now.

2. I'm tired, _____so_____ I'm going to go to bed now.

3. I'm tired, _____and_____ I'm hungry.

4. It's cool outside, _____so_____ I'm going to wear a sweater.

5. It's cool outside, _____but_____ I'm going to wear short pants.

6. It's cool outside, _____and_____ the air feels wonderful.

7. He studied for 4 hours, _____and_____ then he went to bed.

8. He studied for 4 hours, _____but_____ he still didn't understand the lesson.

9. He studied for 4 hours, _____so_____ he passed the quiz today.

10. She is good at all sports, _____but_____ she doesn't like tennis very much.

11. She is good at all sports, _____so_____ she can play tennis and basketball well.

12. She is good at all sports, _____and_____ she is good at languages, too.

Exercise 6. Sentence Study: Details

Read these sentences carefully. Read the question and then circle the letter of the correct answer.

1. Douglas Elton Ulman, who was a famous actor, was born in Denver, Colorado, in 1883.

   When was he born?
   A. in Denver
   B. in 1883
   C. in Colorado
   D. when he was only 18 years old

2. Flamingos live in colonies, and some of these colonies have over a thousand birds.

   How big can some of the groups be?
   A. more than 1,000,000
   B. more than 100,000
   C. more than 10,000
   D. more than 1,000

3. William Faulkner won the Nobel Prize for literature in 1949, and in 1955 he won the Pulitzer Prize for *A Fable* and again in 1963 for *The Reivers*.

   How many times did he win the Nobel Prize for literature?
   A. only one time
   B. two times
   C. three times
   D. none

4. In 1919, Douglas Fairbanks, together with the famous actor Charlie Chaplin, the actress Mary Pickford, and the director D. W. Griffith, started a studio that was called United Artists.

   How many people began the studio with Fairbanks?
   A. three
   B. two
   C. one
   D. none. He did it by himself.

Exercise 7. Sentence Study: Conclusions

Read these sentences carefully. Read the four choices and then circle the letter of the statement that you think is true from the information in the sentences.

1. Beethoven got his first job (as an organ player) when he was only twelve.
   A. He learned to play the organ when he was twelve.
   B. He did not have a job when he was eleven.
   C. The organ was more difficult for him than the violin.
   D. Beethoven made a lot of money at this job.

2. Although Beethoven learned that he was losing his hearing when he was 27, he kept this a secret for a long time.
    A. He could not hear anything when he was 28.
    B. He did not want people to know about this problem.
    C. He had many secrets about his life.
    D. He did not want to learn any more about music.

3. Georgia is the largest state in the eastern half of the United States, but there are twenty other states that are larger.

    A. The larger states are not in the eastern half of the United States.
    B. Georgia is the second largest state in the United States.
    C. There are only twenty large states in the United States.
    D. Half of Georgia is in the eastern part of the United States.

4. A woman came to the door. She said, "I'm sorry to bother you, but I don't have any place to stay."
    A. She wanted some food.
    B. She wanted a room.
    C. She wanted to take a bath.
    D. She wanted something to drink.

Exercise 8. Main Idea

There are two paragraphs in this exercise. Read each paragraph quickly to discover the author's main idea. Read the four possible answers and circle the letter of the one that you think is the main idea. Remember that the main idea is the idea that the whole or complete paragraph discusses.

1. Beethoven was a very famous musical composer. He was born in Germany and grew up there. However, in 1792, Beethoven moved to Vienna, Austria. There he studied with the famous composer Franz Joseph Haydn. Beethoven spent the rest of his life in Austria. He wrote symphonies, operas, and much more there.

    A. Beethoven was not born in Austria, but he lived in several Austrian cities.
    B. In 1792, Beethoven chose to move to Austria.
    C. Austria was a very important place for Beethoven and his work.
    D. Franz Joseph Haydn helped Beethoven to learn a great deal about composing music.

2. William Faulkner was a famous American writer. He was born in a small town in rural Mississippi in 1897. Most of his novels and short stories tell about life in rural Mississippi. Faulkner liked to write about the traditions and history of this area of the American South.

    A. Faulkner was from the American South and wrote about life there.
    B. Faulkner wrote novels and short stories.
    C. Faulkner's first name was William.
    D. Faulkner was born in 1897.

Exercise 9. Organization + Main Idea

There are two paragraphs in this exercise. In each paragraph, there is one sentence that is not related to the main idea or topic of the paragraph. Draw a line through the sentence that does not belong in the paragraph. Then read the four answers and circle the letter of the main idea. Follow the example.

1. California is in the southwest corner of the United States. ~~The weather in this area of the United States is very dry.~~ California is a large state. It has many people. California is now the biggest state in population. There are about 30 million people who live in California. The population of California is growing very quickly.

    (A.) California is a large state with many people in it.
    B. California is in the southwest corner of the United States.
    C. California has more people than New York or Florida.
    D. California is a very large state.

2. One beautiful day a poor man named Ohyo was walking in the mountains. Suddenly he heard a sound. It was a very sad sound. He found a crane (a kind of bird) that was caught in a trap. It couldn't get out. Ohyo felt sorry for the bird, so he helped the crane. He got the crane out of the trap. ~~The trap was made of wood.~~ The crane was hurt, so Ohyo put some medicine on the crane's injury to make it better.

    A. The bird that Ohyo found was a crane.
    (B.) Ohyo helped a bird that he found in the mountains.
    C. The bird did not die, but it cannot fly now.
    D. On the day when the man helped the bird, the weather was beautiful.

Exercise 10. Scanning

Read the two questions and the three answers first. Read the paragraph as quickly as possible to find the answers to the two questions. Circle the letter of your answer.

1. The number of people living in California now is about
    A. 300,000
    (B.) 30,000,000
    C. 130,000,000

2. The two cities mentioned in the paragraph are
    A. Los Angeles and San Diego
    (B.) Los Angeles and San Francisco
    C. Los Angeles and San Jose

    California is in the southwest corner of the United States. California is a large state with several large cities. For example, Los Angeles and San Francisco are in the state of California. California has many people. In fact, California is now the biggest state in population. There are about 30 million people who live in California. The population of California is growing very quickly.

Exercise 11. Sequencing/Prediction

There are four paragraphs in this exercise, but the paragraphs
have been cut into three pieces. Read all the pieces and then
draw a line to connect the three pieces that make a good paragraph. Use one piece from each column (A, B, C) to make
each new paragraph.

A	**B**	**C**
1. The flamingo is a beauti-ful, unique bird. It has a long, curved neck and long, very thin legs.	However, she doesn't think this is a fair rule, so she doesn't pay any attention to the rule.	They are about 4 feet tall. Their feet are shaped like ducks' feet.
2. One of my coworkers smokes in our office. The company has a rule against this.	These are Alabama and Georgia. Florida is a very well-known state. It is famous because the weather is warm.	I've tried to hint that the smoke in the office bothers me, but I have never told her directly that her smoking in the office bothers me. _incomodidad_
3. The state of Florida is in the southeast corner of the United States. Only two other states touch Florida.	It has a curved bill. The color of its feathers can vary from bright red to pale pink.	It is also famous because many international tourists visit Disney World and other places in this state.
4. Douglas Elton Ulman was born in Denver, Colorado, in 1883.	_Maybe_ _Quiza a caso, ta'lvez_ Perhaps you do not know this name. It is possible that you know him by Douglas Fairbanks, his other name.	If you like old movies, maybe you have seen a movie with this actor in it.

STRATEGY 1: Read a Lot!

Read, read, read! The best way for you to improve
your reading in English is to read. Find something
that is interesting to read. Read newspapers,
magazines, and books. Read menus and maps.
Read everything you can!

Exercise 12. Following Directions

Read these instructions and do what they say. Use the space below. You may want to use a pencil for this
exercise so you can erase if you make a mistake. Good luck!

In the box below, draw a large circle.

Now write the letters a, b, c, and d in the places where 3 o'clock, 6 o'clock, 9 o'clock, and 12 o'clock are
    located on a clock. Put a where 3 o'clock would be, b where 6 o'clock would be, c where 9 o'clock
    would be, and d where 12 o'clock would be.

Now draw a line from d to b. Now draw a line from a to c. This line will cut the other line in half.

You now have a round pie that is cut in four pieces. In the piece between points b and c, write your name.
    In the piece between points d and a, write your teacher's name. In the piece between points c and d,
    write your favorite color. In the piece between points a and b, write one kind of food that you hate to
    eat.

Now underline your name. Then circle your teacher's name. Next, draw a big x on the name of the food
    you don't like to eat. Last, draw a rectangle around your favorite color.

Now read all the directions one more time to check your answer.

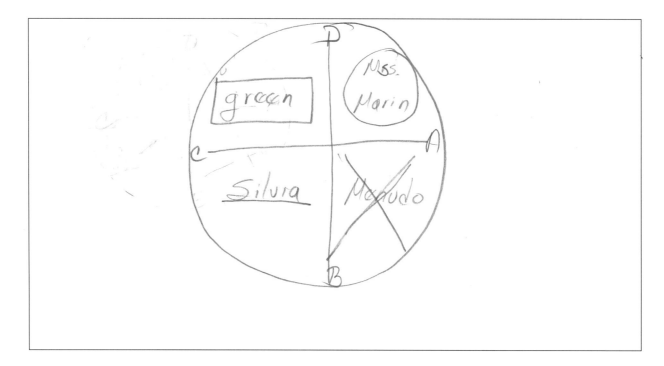

STOP. Do NOT turn the page now. WAIT for your teacher to tell you to begin work.

⟨19⟩

Exercise 13. Timed Word Selection

Directions: Read the word to the left of the line. Then read the five words to the right. Circle the word that is exactly the same as the word to the left of the line.

1. if	in	of	(if)	it	is
2. piece	point	people	pieces	points	(piece)
3. movie	movies	move	(movie)	more	maybe
4. have	(have)	had	has	haven't	hasn't
5. once	one	only	other	old	(once)
6. young	your	you're	year	(young)	just
7. bird	birds	books	book	(bird)	but
8. deal	(deal)	deaf	feel	food	dead
9. below	begin	(below)	began	brown	blow
10. start	state	states	star	stars	(start)
11. year	(year)	your	young	good	fear
12. is	it's	(is)	in	of	if
13. last	late	(last)	letter	list	lost
14. Georgia	Germany	Douglas	corner	George	(Georgia)
15. wanted	wants	(wanted)	worried	worries	want
16. made	many	(made)	mad	makes	make
17. lines	likes	lives	(lines)	limes	lights
18. from	form	for	four	(from)	foot
19. partner	parent	people	(partner)	between	parts
20. was	(was)	well	wasn't	wash	watch
21. smoke	small	short	shoes	(smoke)	secret
22. grew	grow	group	good	year	(grew)
23. many	(many)	more	most	much	man
24. different	difficult	discusses	describe	(different)	differ
25. take	half	have	(take)	make	lake

STOP. Do NOT turn the page.

Exercise 14. Timed Reading

1   Douglas Elton Ulman was born in Denver, Colorado, in 1883. Perhaps you do
2 not know his name. It is possible that you know him by Douglas Fairbanks, his other
3 name. If you like old movies, maybe you have seen a movie with Douglas Fairbanks in it.

4   Douglas Fairbanks was a famous movie star. He made his first movie in 1915.
5 Most of his movies were adventure films. His best movies were silent films. These
6 included *The Mark of Zorro* (1920), *Robin Hood* (1922), *The Thief of Baghdad* (1924),
7 and *The Black Pirate* (1926).

8   In 1919, Fairbanks, together with the famous actor Charlie Chaplin, the actress
9 Mary Pickford, and the director D. W. Griffith, started a studio that was called United
10 Artists. This studio was very important for the American movie industry.

11   In 1920, Fairbanks married Mary Pickford.

1. The main idea of paragraph 2 (lines 4–7) is
     A. Fairbanks made his first movie in 1915
     B. Fairbanks began United Artists studio
     C. Fairbanks made several good movies

2. The word *these* in line 5 means
     A. movies
     B. photographs
     C. stars

3. The reading does not say it, but we can guess that
     A. Fairbanks was a rich man
     B. Pickford was from England
     C. *Robin Hood* was the best movie

4. Which of these happened first?
     A. United Artists was started
     B. Fairbanks married Mary Pickford
     C. *The Mark of Zorro* was made

5. When Fairbanks was about 32 years old, he
     A. got married to Mary Pickford
     B. made the movie *The Black Pirate*
     C. was in his first film

STOP. Do NOT turn the page.

Exercise 15. Timed Word Selection

Directions: Read the word to the left of the line. Then read the five words to the right. Circle the word that is exactly the same as the word to the left of the line.

1. that — this / then / they / (that) / hats
2. Florida — flower / (Florida) / flowers / floods / French
3. found — from / (found) / find / finds / forward
4. ideas — (ideas) / deals / taste / idea / ice
5. people — (people) / piece / points / pieces / point
6. write — writes / wrote / winter / (write) / writing
7. his — her / he's / him / has / (his)
8. famous — farmer / (famous) / family / farther / father
9. your — you / young / (your) / year / yellow
10. small — sell / snail / smell / (small) / smile
11. first — frying / fist / (first) / firm / fills
12. wasn't — (wasn't) / weren't / isn't / aren't / won't
13. this — these / they / that / those / (this)
14. it's — he's / isn't / (it's) / she's / we're
15. read — dear / red / dead / aren't / (read)
16. about — able / (about) / around / allow / aloud
17. thick — think / thinks / (thick) / thirsty / thirty
18. also — (also) / other / shoe / elbow / into
19. there — their / they've / (there) / here / where
20. none — (none) / more / nose / moon / noon
21. choice — choices / chooses / cheese / (choice) / choose
22. writer — wrote / writing / writes / wrong / (writer)
23. thirteen — fourteen / thirty / forty / (thirteen) / thirsty
24. Douglas — Donald / Dennis / Daniel / David / (Douglas)
25. author — artist / (author) / answer / allowing / operator

STOP. Do NOT turn the page.

Exercise 16. Timed Reading

1   The flamingo is a beautiful, unique bird. It has a long, curved neck and long, very
2   thin legs. It has a curved bill. The color of a flamingo's feathers can vary from bright red
3   to pale pink. Most flamingos are about 4 feet tall. Flamingos' feet are shaped like ducks'
4   feet.

5   Flamingos live in colonies or groups. Some of these colonies have over a thousand
6   birds. Flamingos reproduce once a year. The female lays one egg, and for thirty days the
7   parents take turns sitting on the egg. In the wild, flamingos live for fifteen to twenty years.
8   In captivity, they live longer.

9   Flamingos can be found in Africa, Asia, Europe, South America, and the Caribbean
10 area. A long time ago, these birds lived in Florida, but humans killed them to get their
11 colorful feathers.

Flamingo

1. The main idea of paragraph 1 (lines 1–4) is
    A. Florida had many flamingos, but now there are not
        many
    B. the flamingo is a very beautiful and interesting bird
    C. flamingos like to live in large groups

2. The word *pale* in line 3 means
    A. not bright
    B. not bad
    C. not blue

3. The reading does not say it, but we can guess that
    A. flamingos always live in very large groups
    B. flamingos may live a long time in a zoo
    C. flamingos and ducks like to eat different kinds of food

4. A flamingo has legs that are not fat and are not
    A. pink
    B. short
    C. unique

5. The reason that there are no more flamingos in Florida is that
    A. people wanted their feathers
    B. people needed to eat them
    C. both A and B

STOP. Do NOT turn the page.

Exercise 17. Timed Word Selection

Directions: Read the word to the left of the line. Then read the five words to the right. Circle the word that is exactly the same as the word to the left of the line.

1.	helps	(helps)	helped	help	hopes	hoped
2.	two	too	out	(two)	tea	toe
3.	died	lied	(died)	dead	feed	tied
4.	played	plays	playing	(played)	player	play
5.	flamingo	flames	flamingos	farmers	(flamingo)	mango
6.	isn't	don't	aren't	wasn't	it's	(isn't)
7.	happen	(happen)	pepper	paper	happy	happened
8.	quiz	test	guess	(quiz)	question	quiet
9.	tell	tells	tall	(tell)	till	toll
10.	only	once	lonely	alone	one	(only)
11.	correct	collect	(correct)	corner	corners	collects
12.	talk	fork	(talk)	talks	forks	talked
13.	she'll	they'll	he'll	we'll	you'll	(she'll)
14.	smoker	smoked	smoking	smokes	smoke	(smoker)
15.	why	who	when	where	(why)	what
16.	also	(also)	into	under	always	all's
17.	day	dog	dam	(day)	lay	toy
18.	great	greet	(great)	ground	grilled	grand
19.	Florida	(Florida)	France	French	Finland	Florence
20.	where	when	which	whose	(where)	what
21.	famous	(famous)	farmers	fathers	feathers	families
22.	out	our	own	cut	(out)	off
23.	circles	circle	color	circus	colors	(circles)
24.	for	four	(for)	form	far	fur
25.	five	fire	file	fine	(five)	fold

STOP. Do NOT turn the page.

Exercise 18. Timed Reading

1   William Faulkner was a famous American writer. He was born in a small town in
2 rural Mississippi in 1897. Most of his novels and short stories tell about life in rural
3 Mississippi. Faulkner liked to write about the traditions and history of this area of the
4 American South.

5   In his lifetime, Faulkner won many awards for his writings. In 1949, he won the
6 Nobel Prize for literature. In 1955 he won the Pulitzer Prize for *A Fable* and again in 1963
7 for *The Reivers.*

8   Faulkner lived most of his life in Oxford, Mississippi. He traveled a little, but even
9 after he became famous, he still preferred to stay in the small town of Oxford.

10   Once Faulkner described himself as "just a farmer who likes to tell stories."
11 However, he was a very gifted writer with a very special skill.

1. The main idea of paragraph 2 (lines 5–7) is
    A. Faulkner was a very, very good writer
    B. Faulkner was born in a small town
    C. Faulkner was a good writer and a great farmer

2. The word *rural* in line 2 means
    A. not good weather
    B. not a big city
    C. not expensive

3. The reading does not say it, but we can guess that
    A. Faulkner was famous, but he did not change very much
    B. not many people in Oxford knew Faulkner
    C. Faulkner was born in Oxford

4. Which of these is true?
    A. he won the Pulitzer Prize two times
    B. he won the Nobel Prize in 1955
    C. he spoke French and German

5. Most of Faulkner's writing was about
    A. one area of the United States
    B. farmers all over the United States
    C. his travels across the United States

STOP. Do NOT turn the page.

Exercise 19. Timed Word Selection

Directions: Read the word to the left of the line. Then read the five words to the right. Circle the word that is exactly the same as the word to the left of the line.

1. took	take	(took)	cook	look	hook
2. but	bat	boat	bit	(but)	nut
3. month	money	mouth	(month)	north	south
4. office	offer	(office)	off	official	offered
5. out	off	our	(out)	eat	old
6. rule	rail	lost	runs	role	(rule)
7. difficult	(difficult)	different	differed	discuss	discussed
8. between	(between)	below	behind	borrow	bundles
9. wrong	(wrong)	among	write	wrote	wrapped
10. groups	grapes	group	grape	(groups)	ground
11. then	them	this	these	that	(then)
12. off	on	our	own	of	(off)
13. tree	true	towel	time	(tree)	free
14. house	horse	(house)	how's	horses	houses
15. actor	actress	acted	(actor)	artist	acting
16. each	ache	every	peach	teach	(each)
17. well	wall	will	(well)	tell	bell
18. tired	(tired)	tried	tries	tires	tied
19. age	ate	(age)	ache	egg	page
20. born	burn	(born)	burned	barn	barns
21. main	(main)	mail	made	mare	pain
22. really	real	redder	rainy	(really)	rainy
23. helped	helping	helper	helps	help	(helped)
24. organ	only	organs	oddest	(organ)	once
25. people	person	persons	(people)	piece	pieces

STOP. Do NOT turn the page.

Exercise 20. Timed Reading

1   Beethoven's full name was Ludwig van Beethoven. He was born in Bonn,
2 Germany, in 1770. At age five, Beethoven studied the violin, and he soon started with
3 other musical instruments. When he was only twelve, he got his first job as an organ
4 player. He wrote four musical compositions that year.

5   In 1792, Beethoven moved to Vienna, Austria, where he studied with the famous
6 composer Franz Joseph Haydn. Beethoven spent the rest of his life in Austria. He wrote
7 symphonies, operas, and much more.

8   At age 27, Beethoven learned that he was losing his hearing. He kept his
9 deafness a secret for a long time. He became almost totally deaf. In fact, he could
10 only hear his last great works in his imagination because he could not hear at all.
11 Just before he passed away, Beethoven said, "I shall hear in heaven."

1. The main idea of paragraph 1 (lines 1–4) is
    A. Beethoven was good at music when he was very young
    B. Beethoven was born in Germany but lived in Austria
    C. Beethoven studied the violin but was much better as an organ player

2. The word *totally* in line 9 means
    A. a little
    B. sometimes
    C. completely

3. The reading does not say it, but we can guess that
    A. Haydn did not teach Beethoven much
    B. the violin was Beethoven's favorite instrument
    C. Beethoven died in Austria

4. At the end of his career, Beethoven could only hear his music in his head because
    A. he was deaf
    B. he did not have any musical instruments
    C. he died very suddenly

5. The reason that Beethoven moved to Austria was
    A. to study with Haydn
    B. to live outside of Germany
    C. not given in this reading passage

STOP. Do NOT turn the page.

Exercise 21. Timed Word Selection

Directions: Read the word to the left of the line. Then read the five words to the right. Circle the word that is exactly the same as the word to the left of the line.

1. days	stays	dogs	days	dolls	don't
2. cloth	clean	clear	clothing	cloth	clown
3. it	if	it	is	at	of
4. walking	walked	worked	walks	working	walking
5. however	houses	however	whenever	whoever	forever
6. happens	happy	happen	happens	happened	happier
7. crane	crab	cane	rain	crane	cranes
8. folk	yolk	four	folk	fork	talk
9. did	did	didn't	do	doesn't	dad
10. said	said	sad	says	sand	salt
11. if	if	of	us	off	it
12. he's	she's	it's	he's	his	her
13. have	has	had	hats	have	haven't
14. small	smile	smell	shell	small	malls
15. found	find	finds	finding	ground	found
16. not	note	not	nut	notes	ton
17. coworker	coteacher	worker	coworker	teacher	coworke
18. with	wish	with	want	wishes	water
19. should	shell	should	shower	sheep	shoppin
20. things	thinks	think	thirsty	things	thing
21. get	get	got	gas	gold	jet
22. later	late	fatter	latest	laser	later
23. queen	queens	quick	green	quiet	queen
24. make	made	making	Mike	male	make
25. said	said	sad	each	salt	sold

STOP. Do NOT turn the page.

Exercise 22. Timed Reading

1   British Columbia is a province in the western half of Canada. It is the largest
2   province in the western half of Canada, but two other provinces are larger.

3   The weather in the southern half of British Columbia is mild. In fact, it is the
4   mildest in Canada. For this reason, many older people come to live in this area of Canada.

5   There are about three and a half million people living in British Columbia. Only
6   Ontario and Quebec have more people. About half of British Columbia's people originally
7   came from England. Many other people's families came to Canada from Scotland, Ireland,
8   and Germany. Today this province has a higher percentage of Asians than any of the other
9   nine provinces.

10   Vancouver is the largest city in British Columbia. Many international
11   visitors come to Vancouver. They come to see the natural beauty of the coast and the.
12   beautiful mountains. Many ships stop at Vancouver, and it is the largest port in all of
13   Canada.

1. The main idea of paragraph 3 (lines 5–9) is
    A. the people in this province came from many places
    B. not many people from France or Spain came here
    C. there are more Asians in this province than in the
        other provinces

2. The word *port* in line 12 means
    A. a city in the mountains
    B. a city on the coast
    C. a city with many people

3. Manitoba is another province in Canada. The reading does not say it, but we can guess that
    A. British Columbia has more people than Manitoba
    B. Manitoba is warmer than British Columbia
    C. both A and B

4. In population, British Columbia is 3d; in size,
    British Columbia is
    A. 3d
    B. 4th
    C. 9th

5. Vancouver is
    A. the capital of British Columbia
    B. the largest city in British Columbia
    C. both A and B

STOP. Do NOT turn the page.

Exercise 23. Vocabulary Recall

Read the vocabulary word in boldface print on the left. Read the three choices and choose the one that is similar in meaning or has something in common with the first word. Write the letter of the answer on the line.

(22)

		Word	A	B	C
B	1.	award	fighting	prize	no sound
C	2.	population	popular	present	people
A	3.	injury	hurt	great	silent
A	4.	mild	medium	very cold	very hot
B	5.	famous	very sad	well-known	move slowly
B	6.	bother	say	problem	below
C	7.	concerned	tired	wanted	worried
B	8.	square	2 sides	4 sides	6 sides
A	9.	find out	know; learn	clean; wash	do; make
A	10.	literature	read	smoke	start
B	11.	although	and	but	so
B	12.	smell o l u r	big	nose	water
A	13.	none ninguno/nadie	zero	a few	many
C	14.	boss	at home	in school	at work
C	15.	pass away	travel	sell	die
A	16.	agree	say "yes"	think a lot	sleep quickly
B	17.	gifted	not much	good at	presents for
B	18.	round	war	circle	ears
B	19.	deaf sordo	singing	hearing	walking
A	20.	unique	different	difficult	discuss
A	21.	port	coast	river	sky
C	22.	pale	pencils	dishes	colors
B	23.	mention	vary	say	count
A	24.	human	people	music	piece
A	25.	a great deal	a lot	half	reluctant

Explanation for Exercise 1, p. 1:

1. short (You need the opposite of tall.)
2. big, large (You need the opposite of small.)
3. round (A circle is not square. It is round.)
4. old (You need the opposite of new.)
5. rich, wealthy, well-off (You need the opposite of poor.)
6. thin (The opposite of thick is thin.)
7. colorful (Colorful pictures are the opposite of black, white, and gray pictures.)
8. famous, well-known, popular (You need the opposite of not known.)
9. west (also: south, north) (The opposite of east is west, but north and south are possible here.)
10. easy (You need the opposite of difficult.)
11. right, correct (These are the opposite of wrong.)
12. king, president (Many answers are possible. You cannot repeat queen.)
13. same (The opposite of different is same. Also, same *always* uses the: the same.)
14. bad, terrible, horrible (You need the opposite of good.)
15. hates, dislikes, doesn't like (All of these are the opposite of like.)

Lesson 2

Extended Reading Fluency Practices

Exercise 1. Nonprose: Class Schedule

Here is a schedule for the students at the English Language Institute at the University of North Florida. There are three levels: beginning, intermediate, and advanced. Read the schedule and then answer the questions on the next page.

	B1	B2	I1	I2	I3	I4	A1	A2	A3
8:00–8:50	Lab	Gram Jones #102	Gram Lee #103	tutor	Comp Adel #104	Conv Hurt #105	Idioms Scots #106	Read Jenks #107	Gram Gowen #108
9:00–9:50	Voc Conti #101	Conv Lee #108	Voc Turner #107	Gram Adel #105	tutor	Comp Piaf #104	Gram Jones #103	Idioms Scots #102	TOEFL Hurt #106
10:00–10:50	Read Piaf #105	tutor	Read Adel #106	Voc Hurt #102	Gram Jones #101	Read Conti #103	Comp Turner #104	Gram Scots #107	Disc Lee #108
11:00–11:50	Gram Jones #101	Lab	Conv Hurt #103	Read Conti #102	lunch	lunch	Disc Lee #104	lunch	lunch
12:00–12:50	lunch	lunch	lunch	lunch	Voc Lee #105	Gram Turner #106	lunch	Disc Adel #107	Read Piaf #108
1:00–1:50	Conv Adel #101	Voc Hurt #102	Comp Conti #103	Conv Jenks #104	Read Turner #105	tutor	Read Piaf #107	TOEFL Jones #106	Comp Scots #108
2:00–2:50	tutor	Read Turner #102	tutor	Comp Conti #103	Conv Piaf #104	Voc Scots #105	TOEFL Jenks #106	Comp Yee #107	Idioms Masten #108

Key: B: beginning, I: intermediate, A: advanced
Lab: Language Laboratory, Gram: grammar, Comp: composition, Conv: conversation,
Read: reading, Disc: discussion, TOEFL: Test of English as a Foreign Language, Voc: vocabulary
Language laboratory has a native speaker who helps students in the laboratory.
Tutors are native speakers who work with small groups of three to four students at a time.

Notes: Tutor groups will meet at the main office for the first class meeting. The tutor will choose a meeting place for future meetings.
All lab classes will meet in the language laboratory.

Questions for Exercise 1

1. Where do lab classes meet? _In the languague laboratory_

2. What time do beginning students eat lunch? _12:00 to 12:50_

3. How many different classes of students are there at this school? _9 nine_

4. What does Mr. Hurt teach at eight o'clock? _Conversation #105_

5. What does Mrs. Adel teach at one o'clock? _Conversation #101_

6. In what room does group A1 have discussion class? _#104   11:00 to 11:50_

7. Do classes B2 and I3 have lunch together? _No B2 has lunch 12:00 to 12:50 I3 has lunch 11:00 to 11:50_

8. Who teaches TOEFL to class A2? _Mr. Jones_

9. My friend is in class I4. What is my friend's first class every day? _Conversation_

10. Another friend has discussion class after lunch. What class is he in? _A2, Disc. 107_

Now write five original questions of your own. With a partner, take turns asking and answering each other's original questions.

11. _What different classes are there in this school?_

12. _How many 9 nine different times for luchs are there at this school? 2 times 11-11:50 12:00 – 12:50_

13. _What time do beginning students to firts class? 8:00_

14. _What time is the last class for the studens? 2:50_

15. _How tmany different hours for the tutor 1:00 to 1:50 of student are there at this school? 2:00 to 2:50_

STRATEGY 2: Capital Letters

Pay attention to capital letters. There are two general uses for capital letters in English. Capital letters are used at the beginning of every sentence. In addition, we use capital letters for names of people, places, and some things. Examples are George Smith, Vancouver, and IBM.

Exercise 2. Nonfiction: U.S. Map

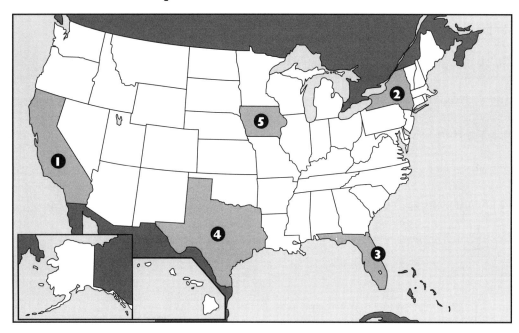

Part 1.   Prereading. Look at the map and try to answer these questions.

1. This is a map of _United   States_.

2. State number 4 is ___Texas___.

3. State number 2 is ___New   York___.

4. Florida is state number ___3___.

5. Have you ever heard the name "Iowa" before?

    Which state do you think is Iowa? number ___5___
    Do you know anything about the state of Iowa? _No_

Part 2.   Look at the map at the top of this page. The reading on pages 24–25 is about this map. Read this information. Write one of these words on the lines:

  Houston, not, name, quickly, state

On the map of the United States above, five states have been shaded. These states are numbered 1, 2, 3, 4, and 5.

    State number 1 is in the southwest corner of the United States. This state is California. California is a large state. California has many people. California is now the biggest state in population. There are about 30 million people who live in California. The population of California is growing very

___quickly___.

State number 2 is in the northeast corner of the map. This state is New York. Many people know New York City. New York City is a large and important city in the state of New York. Both the city and the state have the same _____*name*_____. There are about 18 million people in the state of New York.

State number 3 is in the southeast corner of the United States. This _____*state*_____ is Florida. Florida is a very well-known state. It is famous because the weather is warm. It is also famous because many international tourists visit Disney World and other places in Florida. There are about 13 million people who live in this state.

State number 4 is a very large state, but it is not the biggest state. State number 4 is Texas. Texas is located in the south central part of the United States. The largest cities in Texas are Dallas and _____*Houston*_____. The population of Texas is about 17 million.

State number 5 is in an area of the United States that we call the midwest. (Mid here means middle.) State number 5 is Iowa. Iowa is _____*not*_____ a very big state. The population of Iowa is not very big either. There are about 3 million people in Iowa. Iowa has many farms that give us food. Corn is an important product of Iowa.

Part 3. Outline of the reading. Fill in the missing numbers and words to complete the outline for the reading. Use the words below. (Use one word twice.)

~~Texas~~	~~northeast~~	~~south central~~	3 million
~~population~~	~~30~~	~~Florida~~	~~southeast~~
Iowa	midwest	17 million	location

I. California

   A. Location: southwest

   B. Population: _*30*_ million

II. New York

   A. Location: _*Northeast*_

   B. Population: 18 million

III. _*Florida*_

   A. Location: _*Southeast*_

   B. _*population*_: 13 million

IV. _*Texas*_

   A. Location: _*South Central*_

   B. Population: _*17 million*_

V. _*Iowa*_

   A. _*Location*_ : _*midwest*_

   B. _*population*_ : _*3 million*_

Exercise 3. Fiction

Part 1.   A folktale is a story that people in an area have told and told and told over many years. This folktale is from Japan. It is about a crane, a kind of bird, that helps a man. Read the folktale and answer the questions in the boxes.

A Crane's Payment for a Man's Kindness (583 words)

Once upon a time there was an old man who lived in a small village. This man was very poor. His name was Ohyo. He had a very simple life, but he was very happy.

crane

Question:	Do you know this story already?

One beautiful day he was walking in the mountains. Suddenly he heard a sound. It was a very sad sound. He found a crane that was caught in a trap. It couldn't get out. Ohyo felt sorry for the bird, so he helped the crane. He got the crane out of the trap. The crane was hurt, so Ohyo put some medicine on the crane's injury to make it better.

Question:	What do you think will happen next? Will the crane die?

A few days later, a beautiful woman came to Ohyo's door. "I'm sorry to bother you," she said, "but I don't have any place to stay and it is very late."

When Ohyo saw the woman, it was love at first sight. "You can stay here in my house," he answered. Ohyo loved the woman so much that they got married. They were very happy together, but life was difficult for them because they didn't have any money.

One day the woman made some beautiful cloth for Ohyo. She said, "This cloth will sell for a very high price. I have made this to help you."

Question:	What do you think the cloth was made of?

Ohyo took the cloth to the market to sell it. He was very surprised when he was able to get a lot of money for the cloth. He asked his wife to make some more cloth. At first, she was reluctant to do this. Then Ohyo talked to her about this for a long time. "Please, please, please make some more cloth for me," he asked. Finally she agreed to do this for him. However, she said there was one very important special condition.

"I will make more cloth for you," said his wife, "but you must promise me one simple thing."

"Yes, anything," said Ohyo.

"Whatever happens, you must never look at me while I am making the cloth. Never. Do you understand this?" she asked. "Can you promise this?"

Question:	Do you think this condition is strange?

Ohyo quickly agreed. He was so happy that she was going to make more cloth, and her promise was such a simple one.

Question:	Why do you think Ohyo agreed to this condition so quickly?

Everything was fine. Ohyo was happy because his wife continued to make more cloth. He sold the cloth for a lot of money in the marketplace. Life was good.

Question:	What do you think will happen next?

Ohyo wanted to see how his wife could make such beautiful cloth. He remembered his promise not to look at his wife when she was making the cloth. One day, however, Ohyo could not stop himself. The door to the room where his wife was working was open a little. He walked to the door very quietly. He looked inside the room. He was so surprised.

He did not see his wife making the cloth. He was surprised because he saw the crane that he had helped several months before. The crane was making the beautiful cloth from its beautiful feathers.

Question:	Who was making the cloth? Where was his wife?

The crane heard the door move. The crane saw Ohyo. "I am the crane that you helped. When I was in trouble, you helped me. I wanted to pay you back for your kindness, so I made this beautiful cloth for you. However, now you know who I am, so I cannot stay here any longer."

In that moment, the crane flew out the window. Ohyo was in the room crying "Please don't leave. Please don't go. I'm sorry."

It was too late. The crane was already gone.

Question:	Does this story have a happy ending?

Part 2.   Sometimes a folktale has a moral. A moral means a kind of teaching. The story can teach us something important about life.

What is the moral of this story? _____

_____

_____

_____

Discuss your answer in small groups.

Part 3.   Summary Practice. Read this summary of the folktale. The folktale has 583 words, but this summary has only 185 words. Some of the words are missing. Fill in the blanks with a correct word.

Summary of "A Crane's Payment for a Man's Kindness"

"A Crane's Payment for a Man's Kindness" is a folktale from Japan. In this story, a poor man named Ohyo (1) _found_ / _heard_ a crane in the mountains one day. The crane was hurt, and (2) _he_ helped the crane. A few days later, a beautiful woman came to Ohyo's (3) _house_ looking for a place to stay. Ohyo fell in love with (4) _her_ at once. Soon they were married. They had a good life, but (5) _they_ did not have much money. The wife decided to help their (6) _situation_ by making a very special cloth that Ohyo sold in the (7) _market_ for a large amount of money. The wife agreed to make this (8) _cloth_ if Ohyo promised not to look at her when she was making it. Everything was OK, but one (9) _time_ Ohyo looked at his wife while she was making the special cloth. However, he did not see his (10) _wife_. He saw the crane that he had helped before. The crane (11) _said_ that she had to leave because Ohyo had looked at her when she was making the cloth. Ohyo was very (12) _sad_ to lose his beautiful wife.

Exercise 4. News Reports: True or False?

Read these three news stories. Two of them are false and one of them is true. Circle true or false. Then answer the question at the end of this exercise.

1. true or false?   **Americans Want a King**

In the United States, there is a president, but in England there is a queen and in Spain there is a king. *Newsweek* magazine asked 400 Americans this question: Should the United States have a president as now, or should the United States have a king or a queen? The answers were very surprising. About 45% said we should have a president. The really surprising point of this survey was that about 40% wanted to have a king or a queen. About 15% said that we should only have a queen. Although these numbers are important, no one really believes that the U.S. government will change the system in the near future.

2. true or false? **Chimpanzee Speaks English**

At a science laboratory near San Francisco, California, scientists have found out something very important. They have trained a chimpanzee named Jo-Jo to speak. Jo-Jo, age 3, can actually say about seven expressions in English. These expressions include: "I'm sorry," "Where are you going?" and "I'm hungry." In the past, other chimpanzees were able to communicate using pictures, sign language, or computers, but this is the first time that anyone has been able to train a chimpanzee to speak with human beings.

3. true or false? **A Dangerous Sport**

Can you name a sport that is dangerous? Perhaps your answer is football. Maybe you said boxing. Perhaps you said skiing. What about Ping-Pong? Not many people would say that Ping-Pong is a dangerous sport. However, according to a government report in 1992, over 1,450 people had to go to the emergency room at a hospital after they played Ping-Pong. That's right — Ping-Pong!

I think number _true_ is true because _the people went to play only see the ball and this will to provocke an accident went their move. Some times how ever went to lance the ball estrong to provoke damage to the muscles, arms, The people thinking about this sport is easy but to confide provoke accident during the t_

STRATEGY 3:
Periods (.) and Question Marks (?)

Look carefully for the periods and question marks. We use periods and question marks at the end of sentences. Practice: Look at "Americans Want a King," on page 28. How many sentences are there in that paragraph?

Exercise 5. Reading/Discussion/Writing: Smoking at Work

Part 1.   Read this letter from a person who has a problem with a coworker. Then work with a classmate
to discuss your answers to the questions after the letter.

> *Dear Advisor,*
>
> *I've got a problem with one of my coworkers and I just don't know what to do. I
> work at a large company. In the office where I work, there are four people who share
> the office area. Of course we each have our own desk, telephone, etc., but we share
> the same air and that is the problem.*
>
> *One of my coworkers smokes in the office. The company has a rule against this,
> but my coworker doesn't think this is a fair rule so she doesn't pay any attention to the
> rule. I've tried to hint that the smoke in the office bothers me, but I have never told
> her directly that her smoking in the office bothers me. I'm not making any progress
> with this strategy.*
>
> *I've talked to my other two coworkers. Neither of them smokes, but the smoke in
> the office air does not bother them. They don't care if anyone smokes in the office or
> not.*
>
> *I'm concerned about my health. I hear more and more news that "secondhand"
> smoke is unhealthy. I don't like the fact that my hair and my clothes stink of cigarette
> smoke when I leave the office every day.*
>
> *What should I do?*
>
> *Chris*

Part 2.   Discuss your answers to these questions with a classmate.

1. What is Chris's problem?
2. Do you think that Chris has a real problem? Why or why not?
3. Have you ever experienced this problem before? Where and when?
4. What do you think Chris should do?

Part 3. Now read these responses from four different people. Which response do you think is the best? Why? Which one is the worst? Why do you think this?

Answer 1

Dear Chris,

I'm a smoker, and I'm tired of you nonsmokers trying to run our lives. If we smokers want to smoke, it's our right. Who are you to tell us not to smoke? I don't tell you what to do in your life, so what gives you the right to tell me what to do? This is crazy.

Leave your coworker alone! Don't bother her with this silly issue. It sounds to me that everyone in the office is getting along fine—except for you! Perhaps you are the problem, not your coworkers!

Think about it, Chris!

Rachel

smoker
troublemaker
stubbor
selfish
crazy
angry
aggresive/neg.
lonely
negative

Answer 2

Dear Chris,

What are you waiting for? Talk to your coworker about this problem. Tell her that she has to stop smoking in the office. It's the rule in most companies. Everyone has to follow the rules.

Of course smoking is bad for you. I hate that cigarette smoke smell in my clothes, too.

Good luck with this situation.

Pamela

- understanding
- not afraid
- do it yourself
- secure
- positive
- get involved/advice
- agresive/positive

Answer 3

Dear Chris,

Talk to your boss. If there is a rule in your company against smoking in a common area, then your boss should take care of the situation. It's not your job to do this. Let someone higher up take care of this problem.

I hope you get some clean air soon!

Zina

- smart/professional
- take a control
- correct method
- someone else deal with the problem
- don't get involved
- polite

Answer 4

Dear Chris,

Forget it. If you talk to your coworker, nothing will change. She knows the rule now but smokes anyway. If you talk to her, she'll get angry.

If you talk to your boss, he will think you are a troublemaker. You can't win in this situation.

Life is not fair, is it?

Carrine

[handwritten annotations:]
- Angry
- give up / quitter
- nothing will change
- pessimist
- no hope

Part 4.   For homework, write your own reply letter to Chris. Follow the four examples in part 3. Write your own opinion. Try to limit your answer to 125 words. Be sure to say EXACTLY what you think Chris should do. Be sure to give reasons why Chris should follow your suggestion.

At the next class, pass around your papers so that everyone gets to read everyone else's letters.

Lesson 3

Exercises and Skills Practices

Exercise 1. Context Clues: Descriptions

Complete each sentence with your own words. Then discuss your answers with a partner or with your class. There may be no single best answer at times. Possible answers are on page 53.

1. On our trip to New York, we visited an art _Museums_ *Academy Gallery* . In this place, we were able to see many famous paintings. Some of these paintings were very old.

2. A man keeps his money and credit cards in his wallet, but a woman usually has a _purse_ _handbag._ .

3. The plane leaves in 15 minutes. If we don't _hurry_ , we'll be late and miss the plane!

4. John didn't want anyone to steal his car, so he has a special

   alarm in it. If anyone touches the door of his car, there is a loud sound to attract people's attention.

5. George Washington was the first _President_ of the United States. People who have had this job recently were Jimmy Carter, George Bush, and Bill Clinton.

George Washington
1732-1982
USA 20c

6. We like to go to that beach because the water is so blue and the

   sand is so white.

7. If you need a book for your class, go to the _library_ . There are thousands of books there and they are open from 9 A.M. to 8 P.M. The best time to go there is when it is quiet in the early morning because there are not so many young children there then.

8. It is sometimes difficult to drive today's large cars on some of the old

   bridges because the bridges are so _narrow_ *side* . This is because the bridges were built for only one car at a time.

a bridge

9. I eat breakfast at that restaurant every morning because they have

   newspapers from all over the United States. These newspapers are _free_ . We don't have to pay anything for them.

10. The human body has 206 _bones_ in it. We need these to help us to keep our shape. Without these, we could not sit up or move at all.

33

Exercise 2. Context Clues

In each of these sentences, you will find an italicized word or group of words. Read the three choices and then decide which choice means about the same as the italicized word or words. Circle the letter of your answer.

1. Lou Gehrig had a very serious *disease*. In 1939, he died from this *disease*.
   A. bad news
   B. sickness
   C. difficulty

2. In 1638, John Harvard *donated* some money and about four hundred books to a new university. The gift was so important that the university was named for John Harvard.
   A. gave
   B. liked
   C. made

3. President John Kennedy was *assassinated* in 1963. President Anwar Sadat of Egypt was also *assassinated*. This was a great loss for both countries.
   A. liked
   B. killed
   C. chosen by the people

4. In the United States, most workers *retire* when they become 65 years old.
   A. work well
   B. stop working
   C. make a lot of money

5. Numbers that are in *consecutive* order are easy to remember.
   A. 1 2 3 4 5 6 7
   B. 9 4 2 8 1 3 5
   C. 1 0 5 9 7 2 2

6. I wake up when my alarm clock *goes off*. If it doesn't *go off*, I can't wake up.
   A. makes noise
   B. costs a lot of money
   C. has numbers on the face

Exercise 3. Context Clues + Dictionary Work

In each of these sentences, you will find an italicized word or group of words. Read the sentence and then write your guess about the meaning of the word. Then look up the word in a dictionary and write the real meaning.

1. Carol Wood was a famous *author* of children's books. Although she died many years ago, children still love to read her books today.

   YOUR GUESS: _how Person writes the book._

   REAL MEANING: _She writes Children's book._

2. Penguins are very interesting birds. They _lay_ only one egg.

    YOUR GUESS: _Put place_

    REAL MEANING: _to put something down carefully_

3. When the egg _hatched,_ the baby bird came out of the egg.

    YOUR GUESS: _it breaks, letting the young bird_

    REAL MEANING: _broke out_

4. She was a famous writer. In her books, she used people that she knew as _models_ for the people in her books.

    YOUR GUESS: _Someone you should imitate because of their good qualities._

    REAL MEANING: _____

5. I didn't study last night and we had a big test this morning in my first class. _Fortunately_ for me, the questions were very easy and I passed the test.

    YOUR GUESS: _happening because of good luck._

    REAL MEANING: _lucky_

6. It is easy to find a blue car or a white car, but an orange car is _rare_.

    YOUR GUESS: _not happen very often_

    REAL MEANING: _extrange, almost never,_

7. Kevin read the _entire_ story, but Ken only read the first page.

    YOUR GUESS: _the entire period of time_

    REAL MEANING: _____

8. The only _enemy_ of the giraffe is the lion. Lions kill giraffes for food.

    YOUR GUESS: _Someone who hates you hand wants to harm you_

    REAL MEANING: _Oposit a like,_

9. Human beings, monkeys, cats, and kangaroos are _mammals_. Snakes, birds, fish, and turtles are not _mammals_.

    YOUR GUESS: _Milk of the mother_

    REAL MEANING: _Not from the mother reprodotion for eggs_

10. The _source_ of this river is very high in those mountains. The water travels all the way from those mountains to the Atlantic Ocean.

    YOUR GUESS: _origen_

    REAL MEANING: _to find out where something can be obtained from._

11. The airplane crashed. There were 100 people on the plane. The news on TV said that 42 people died in the crash. However, 58 people _survived_.

    YOUR GUESS: _____

    REAL MEANING: _the state of continuing to live or exist._

12. I wrote a letter to Mr. Green last month, but I have not received a _reply_ from him. I hope his answer comes soon.

    YOUR GUESS: _answer_

    REAL MEANING: _to answer someone by saying or writing something_

    Carol Kinney
    4 Main St.
    America, US 55012

    Mr. Robert Green
    56 E. 108th St. #12
    Wakazuma, AL 99012

Exercise 4. Language Focus: Pronouns

Each paragraph has one connector. Read the paragraph and then choose which of the pronouns is correct. Underline the correct pronoun and then circle the word that it refers to.

1. In the United States, every child had a free education. This idea soon led to free libraries. One of the first libraries that used tax money to buy books was a (library) in Peterborough, New Hampshire. (It, He, She, They, I) was set up in 1833.

2. Lou Gehrig was a very famous baseball player. In fact, (it, he, they, I, she) was one of the greatest players of all time. Between 1925 and 1929, Gehrig played 2,130 consecutive games for the New York Yankees.

3. Penguins live in large flocks, or groups. (It, He, She, They, I) move very, very slowly on land. However, (it, he, she, they, I) can move very fast under the water or on top of the water. Penguins have very few natural enemies.

   USA
   29

   King Penguins

4. Jane Austen wrote six books. Two of (her, it, us, them, me) were published after her death in 1817. Perhaps the most famous of (her, it, us, them, me) is _Pride and Prejudice_.

5. The American Civil War began in 1861. Who was President when (it, he, she, they, I) began? Was it George Washington or Abraham Lincoln?

6. The giraffe is the tallest animal that is alive today. (It, He, She, They, I) has a very, very long neck.

7. Good morning, sir. My name is Officer Underhill and (it, he, she, they, I) am here to investigate the theft of the painting. What can you tell me about (it, him, her, them, me)?

Exercise 5. Language Focus: Pronouns

Each of the sentences has a blank. Complete the sentence by writing the correct pronoun on the line. Sometimes more than one answer is possible. Then circle the noun that the pronoun refers to in the sentence.

example: (Lou Gehrig) was a famous baseball player. _____He_____ retired from baseball in 1939.

1. Thomas Bray began the first free lending library in the late 1600s. ____He____ began more than 30 of these libraries in the American colonies.

2. In a subscription library, people pay money to become members at first, but ____they____ may borrow the books without paying again.

3. Penguins are special birds. ____They____ cannot fly. ____They____ have very narrow wings and special feathers.

4. There are many kinds of penguins, but all of ____them____ live in the southern half of the world. Most of them live on Antarctica.

5. The flag of the United States has 13 stripes. Seven of ____them____ are red; the others are white.

6. Lou Gehrig was a very famous baseball player. In fact, ____He____ was one of the greatest players of all time.

7. The blue box in the upper left-hand corner of the flag contains

    50 white stars. ____It____ has one star for each of the states.

8. Jane Austen was born in Hampshire, England, in 1775.

    ____She____ was the youngest child in her family. ____They____ lived in a very small town.

9. When one parent gets tired, ____he____ or ____she____ passes the egg to the other parent from foot to foot.

10. After the egg hatches, that is, the baby comes out of the egg, ____It____ continues to stay by the parents' feet.

U.S. Flag

STRATEGY 4:
Paragraphs and Indentation

A reading is divided into several paragraphs. Each paragraph has several sentences. Each paragraph has one main idea. A paragraph begins with an indentation. Practice: Look at the reading on page 50. How many paragraphs are there?

4 paragraphs

Exercise 6. Sentence Study: Details

Read these sentences carefully. Read the question and then circle the letter of the correct answer.

1. In a subscription library, people pay money to become members, but they may borrow the books without paying again.

    When do people pay for this library?
    A. only at the beginning
    B. every time they use the library
    C. when they want to read a book
    D. this kind of library is free

2. Jane Austen, who was the youngest child in her family, was born in Hampshire, England, in 1775.

    How many brothers and sisters did Austen have?
    A. more than three
    B. two or three
    C. only one
    D. the answer is not given

3. Lou Gehrig, who began playing for the New York Yankees in 1923, stopped playing in 1939 because he was very sick.

    In what year did Lou Gehrig start his career for the New York team?
    A. 1923
    B. 1924
    C. 1939
    D. 1940

4. The two police officers who had been looking around in another room walked into the main room where the four people were standing.

    How many people are in the main room now?
    A. six
    B. four
    C. two
    D. none

Exercise 7. Sentence Study: Conclusions

Read these sentences carefully. Read the four choices and then circle the letter of the statement that you think is true from the information in the sentences.

1. Penguins move very, very slowly on land. However, they can move very fast under the water or on top of the water.
    A. They are warmer on land than in the water.
    B. It is more dangerous when they are on land.
    C. Penguins cannot fly and they cannot swim well.
    D. These animals can move faster under the water than on top of the water.

2. The flag of that country has thirteen stripes: seven are red and the others are white.
    A. Some of the stripes are blue.
    B. Six of the stripes are white.
    C. Twenty-three of the stripes are white.
    D. There are twenty-three stripes on the flag.

3. There are many kinds of penguins, but all of them live in the southern half of the world.
    A. This kind of penguin only lives in one part of the world.
    B. There are no penguins that live in the northern half of the world.
    C. Some of the penguins live in the north; the others live in the south.
    D. The penguins in the north are not the same as the penguins in the south.

4. The blue box in the upper left-hand corner of the flag contains fifty white stars, and there is one star for each of the states.
    A. The white stars are in the blue box.
    B. When there were only thirty states, there were fifty stars on the flag.
    C. The blue box is next to the stars.
    D. There are some blue stars in the white box.

Exercise 8. Main Idea

There are two paragraphs in this exercise. Read each paragraph quickly to discover the author's main idea. Read the four possible answers and circle the letter of the one that you think is the main idea. Remember that the main idea is the idea that the whole or complete paragraph discusses.

1. Jane Austen wrote six books. Two of these books were published after her death in 1817. Her other four books did not have her name on them. At that time, it was not considered proper for women to write books, so she could not put her own name on the books that she wrote. Perhaps the most famous of her books is *Pride and Prejudice*.

    A. Austen's best book is *Pride and Prejudice*.
    B. Austen could not put her real name on her books.
    C. Some of Austen's books were published after her death.
    D. Jane Austen was a famous author.

2. The first flag of the United States was chosen on June 14, 1777, by the Continental Congress. However, no one knows for sure who made the first flag. Francis Hopkinson said that he had designed the first flag. In 1870, William Canby said that his grandmother, Betsy Ross, had made the first American flag. We do not know if either is true.

    A. The origin of the flag of the United States is not clear.
    B. Most people believe that Betsy Ross made the first U.S. flag.
    C. The flag of the United States was chosen on June 14, 1777.
    D. Francis Hopkinson did not know William Canby or Betsy Ross.

Exercise 9. Organization + Main Idea

There are two paragraphs in this exercise. In each paragraph, there is one sentence that is not related to the main idea or topic of the paragraph. Draw a line through the sentence that does not belong in the paragraph. Then read the four answers and circle the letter of the main idea.

White Bengal Tiger

1. In Syracuse, New York, police were surprised when they went to the home of Vincent Pace. The police found 74 animals inside the house. These animals included an African lion, an Indian tiger, and an Australian wallaby. An African lion is much stronger than an Indian tiger. This was a problem because many of the animals were protected animals. It is against the law for people to own these animals. Pace said that he had done nothing wrong. He said that he took care of the animals, that the animals were in good shape, and that he gave them to new owners.

   A. A man got into trouble because he had a lot of protected animals in his house.
   B. The police did not want to look for the animals because they were protected.
   C. A man said he was taking care of all the animals that were in his house.
   D. The animals in the man's house were a lion, a tiger, and a wallaby.

2. My good friend Theo and I are in the same history class at school. We have a big test tomorrow, and Theo has a copy of the test. The test has 40 questions. He told me that he will give me a copy of the test if I want one. I don't know what to do. I know that this is cheating, and I know that cheating is wrong. However, a lot of people in my class will see the copy of the test, so I might be the only person who does not look at it. Also, I am very worried about my grade in this class, and history is my worst subject.

   A. The writer's friend does not like to study history.
   B. History is the writer's worst subject in school.
   C. The writer does not know what to do now about this situation.
   D. Many people in the class might look at the test before tomorrow.

Exercise 10. Scanning

Read the two questions and the three answers first. Read the paragraph as quickly as possible to find the answers to the two questions. Circle the letter of your answer.

1. In 1927, the number of home runs that Babe Ruth hit was

   A. 27
   B. 47
   C. 60

2. In 1923,

   A. Gehrig was born in New York City
   B. Gehrig became a member of the New York Yankees team
   C. Gehrig hit many home runs

   Henry Louis Gehrig was born in New York City. He began playing on a professional team in 1923. That team was the New York Yankees. He played first base. Although Gehrig played very well, he was not as famous as his teammate Babe Ruth. In 1927, Lou Gehrig hit 47 home runs. This number was very good, but Babe Ruth hit 60 home runs in the same year.

Exercise 11. Sequencing/Prediction

There are four paragraphs in this exercise, but the paragraphs have been cut into three pieces. Read all the pieces and then draw a line to connect the three pieces that make a good paragraph. Use one piece from each column (A, B, C) to make each new paragraph.

A	**B**	**C**
1. The flag of the United States has thirteen stripes. Seven of these are red.	You have to tell the truth, 100% of the truth. Talk to your teacher about this.	This box contains fifty white stars. There is one star for each of the states.
2. Just then a woman came into the museum. She quickly began to speak.	Sometimes a giraffe is able to kill a lion by kicking it.	With a very surprised look on her face, she continued talking. "What is going on here?" she asked.
3. I think you have to tell your teacher that your friend Theo has a copy of the test.	"Oh, Mr. Nix, I'm sorry to be late again, but —" Just then she saw the policeman and her voice stopped for a moment.	Another enemy, unfortunately, is man. People have taken land for farms, forcing the giraffes to leave the area.
4. Giraffes use their strong legs and feet to protect themselves. Their only natural enemy is a lion.	The others are white. There is a blue box in the top left-hand corner of the flag.	If you don't want to do this, then perhaps you can write a letter to your teacher without signing your name on it.

Exercise 12. Following Directions

Read these instructions and do what they say. Use the space below. You may want to use a pencil for this exercise so you can erase if you make a mistake. Good luck!

In the box below, draw two vertical lines. This will make three new boxes that are the same size.
Then draw a horizontal line through the middle of all the boxes. This will make six new boxes that are the same size.
In the top right box, print your own name.
In the bottom left box, answer this question: "What month were you born in?"
In the box in the top middle, draw a circle.
In the box under where your name is, write your favorite vegetable.
In the bottom middle box, answer this question: "What is your favorite sport to watch?"
In the last box, draw a triangle.
Now draw another circle inside the circle that you have now.
Now write the first letter of your last name inside the inner circle.
Draw a big X across the box that does not have any letters in it.

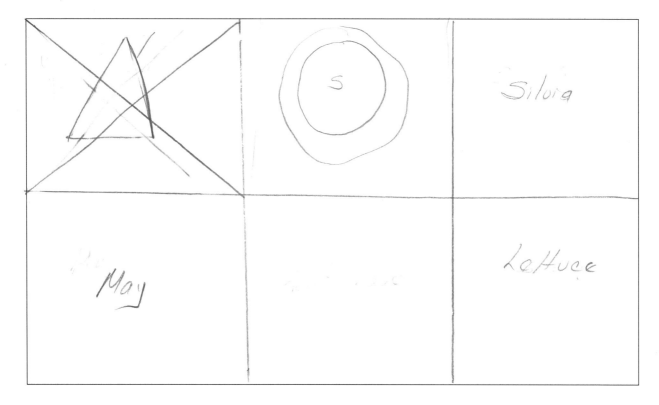

STOP. Do NOT turn the page now. WAIT for your teacher to tell you to begin work.

Exercise 13. Timed Word Selection

Directions: Read the word to the left of the line. Then read the five words to the right. Circle the word that is exactly the same as the word to the left of the line.

1.	about	always	also	above	agree	(about)
2.	blue	(blue)	blood	black	glue	true
3.	either	eastern	neither	(either)	feather	faster
4.	city	cities	(city)	stay	silly	cool
5.	first	fast	faster	fist	feast	(first)
6.	John	Jack	June	Jane	(John)	jump
7.	liked	likes	like	alike	(liked)	linked
8.	public	puddle	(public)	bubble	poodle	under
9.	team	time	(team)	meat	tame	steam
10.	these	(these)	those	that's	there	them
11.	author	artist	article	although	authors	(author)
12.	child	(child)	hill	chill	hide	China
13.	buy	buys	bought	boys	boy	(buy)
14.	difficult	different	disease	(difficult)	diseases	offer
15.	more	move	some	Rome	most	(more)
16.	name	mean	main	(name)	names	named
17.	used	uses	(used)	using	user	use
18.	they	them	they	stay	days	this
19.	ended	ended	ending	ends	endings	sender
20.	rare	real	rare	are	roar	room
21.	small	smell	small	smile	malls	smiles
22.	idea	ideas	area	areas	idle	idea
23.	however	whenever	whoever	however	wherever	whether
24.	books	books	book	banks	bank	boots
25.	after	always	also	after	feather	afraid

STOP. Do NOT turn the page.

Exercise 14. Timed Reading

1   In 1638, John Harvard donated some money and about four hundred books to a
2   new university. This was the beginning of the library at Harvard University. The gift was
3   so important that the university was named for John Harvard.

4   Thomas Bray began the first free lending library in the late 1600s. He set up more
5   than 30 of these libraries in the American colonies. However, the idea for this kind of free
6   library ended when Bray died in 1730. In 1731, Benjamin Franklin and some friends
7   started the first subscription library in the United States. In a subscription library, people
8   pay money to become members, but they may borrow the books without paying again.

9   In the United States, every child had a free education. This idea soon led to free libraries.
10   One of the first libraries that used tax money to buy books was a library in Peterborough,
11   New Hampshire. This library was set up in 1833.

1. The main idea of paragraph 2 (lines 4–8) is
    A. Franklin started the first subscription library
    B. Bray and Franklin were important in the history of public libraries
    C. Bray died in 1730 and Franklin died in 1833

2. The word *borrow* in line 8 means
    A. read and write with no help from another person
    B. use for a short time and then return
    C. like very much

3. The reading does not say it, but we can guess that
    A. there were free schools in the United States before there were
        free libraries
    B. free schools and free libraries in the United States began at about
        the same time
    C. the library in New Hampshire also had a free school in it

4. Harvard University began
    A. in 1638
    B. in 1730
    C. in 1833

5. At the library that Franklin started,
    A. children could use books for no money at all
    B. people paid a little money in the beginning but none after that
    C. both A and B

STOP. Do NOT turn the page.

Exercise 15. Timed Word Selection

Directions: Read the word to the left of the line. Then read the five words to the right. Circle the word that is exactly the same as the word to the left of the line.

1. died	dead	(died)	deal	diet	tied
2. colors	color	coming	(colors)	collars	collar
3. said	sand	(said)	says	saying	sail
4. flock	flood	film	flags	flocks	(flock)
5. start	stars	star	starts	started	(start)
6. wrote	write	where	road	(wrote)	would
7. every	ever	very	(every)	even	event
8. but	(but)	ban	bump	put	pun
9. area	are	real	rear	arena	(area)
10. age	(age)	ago	ice	ore	old
11. game	games	(game)	names	name	gone
12. other	others	allow	bother	(other)	oven
13. penguin	purpose	pencil	(penguin)	penguins	purposes
14. could	couldn't	would	should	(could)	wouldn't
15. move	more	most	(move)	moon	stove
16. free	flee	tree	fried	Fred	free
17. protect	publish	public	protect	protects	publishes
18. young	younger	young	year	years	yours
19. disease	different	difficult	diseases	disease	death
20. June	June	John	Jean	July	Joan
21. by	be	to	at	my	by
22. any	many	ant	any	only	icy
23. famous	feet	find	feather	farmers	famous
24. wings	wing	wind	wings	swing	wigs
25. time	tips	team	timer	times	time

STOP. Do NOT turn the page.

Exercise 16. Timed Reading

1   Penguins are special birds. They cannot fly. They have very narrow wings and
2 special feathers. There are many kinds of penguins, but all of them live in the southern half
3 of the world. Most of them live on Antarctica.

4   Penguins live in large flocks, or groups. They move very, very slowly on land.
5 However, they can move very fast under the water or on top of the water. They have very
6 few natural enemies.

7   King penguins are one type of penguin. They are interesting because they lay only
8 one egg. One of the parents keeps the egg on one of its feet. The parents have extra skin
9 that hangs down to protect the egg. When one parent gets tired, he or she passes the egg to
10 the other parent from foot to foot. After the egg hatches, that is, the baby comes out of the
11 egg, the baby continues to stay by the parents' feet.

1. The main idea of paragraph 3 (lines 7–11) is
    A. king penguin parents both take care of the egg
    B. baby king penguins like to stay near their parents after they are born
    C. the way that king penguins raise their young is interesting

2. The word *flocks* in line 4 means
    A. flies
    B. areas of water
    C. groups

3. The reading does not say it, but we can guess that
    A. penguins do not live in Alaska, Russia, or Canada
    B. penguins can fly in the air but not very well
    C. penguin eggs are very, very light and can break very easily

4. The wings of a penguin are
    A. usually black on top and white on the bottom
    B. not very wide
    C. able to move to the left and to the right

King Penguins

5. It is difficult to find
    A. a group of penguins
    B. a penguin living by itself
    C. two baby penguins from the same mother

STOP. Do NOT turn the page.

15

Exercise 17. Timed Word Selection

Directions: Read the word to the left of the line. Then read the five words to the right. Circle the word that is exactly the same as the word to the left of the line.

1. box	(box)	boxes	but	buy	buys
2. join	jeans	(join)	coin	coins	John
3. people	person	purple	(people)	played	parent
4. stars	start	(starts)	rats	stars	star
5. world	would	wind	word	words	(world)
6. king	kind	gift	fight	knife	(king)
7. began	begin	become	behind	(began)	begun
8. flag	flat	flap	(flag)	glad	flow
9. others	always	other	(others)	ones	another
10. some	same	(some)	come	game	gone
11. states	(states)	state	stays	stay	steaks
12. very	every	even	vertical	vary	(very)
13. for	four	(for)	fur	far	her
14. air	hair	ear	(air)	aid	aim
15. however	whoever	(however)	whenever	everyone	wherever
16. either	eastern	teacher	neither	painter	either
17. read	road	reads	roads	read	earth
18. finds	find	finds	minds	mind	winds
19. is	it	as	us	is	it's
20. person	people	person	purple	purpose	purposes
21. could	could	couldn't	would	wouldn't	called
22. children	child	brothers	parents	children	sister
23. but	bat	bet	bit	buy	but
24. money	many	monkey	money	monkeys	marry
25. likes	likes	liked	lights	limes	lids

STOP. Do NOT turn the page.

Exercise 18. Timed Reading

1   Jane Austen was a famous author. Her books are very popular all over the world.

2   Austen was born in Hampshire, England, in 1775. She was the youngest child in
3 her family. She lived in a very small town, and she was very interested in the people and
4 things there. She began writing at a very early age. She used people that she knew as
5 models for the characters in her books. This explains why her books seem very real and
6 are interesting to so many people even today.

7   Jane Austen wrote six books. Two of these books were published after her death
8 in 1817. Her other four books did not have her name on them. At that time, it was not
9 considered proper for women to write books, so she could not put her own name on the
10 books that she wrote. Perhaps the most famous of her books is *Pride and Prejudice*.

1. The main idea of paragraph 2 (lines 2–6) is
    A. the author was born in England, so she wrote in the English language
    B. the author liked to write about children and places that we like today
    C. the author started to write interesting stories when she was very young

2. The word *proper* in line 9 means
    A. clean
    B. correct
    C. sometimes

3. The reading does not say it, but we can guess that
    A. Austen never saw a book with her name on it
    B. *Pride and Prejudice* was published before 1817
    C. we cannot find any book with the author's name Austen
       on it

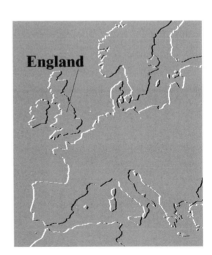

England

4. The number of books that Austen wrote was
    A. 2
    B. 6
    C. 7

5. Austen tried to write about
    A. real people
    B. life in an American town
    C. very young children

STOP. Do NOT turn the page.

Exercise 19. Timed Word Selection

Directions: Read the word to the left of the line. Then read the five words to the right. Circle the word that is exactly the same as the word to the left of the line.

1.	wrote	write	(wrote)	writing	writes	rotten
2.	use	used	(use)	uses	fuse	music
3.	well	wall	will	when	wetter	(well)
4.	model	money	many	modern	(model)	made
5.	eggs	(eggs)	egg	legs	leg	sell
6.	died	dies	tied	dead	die	(died)
7.	career	carry	(career)	common	cancer	called
8.	by	be	(by)	boy	buy	my
9.	all	call	ill	(all)	art	old
10.	in	on	(in)	an	is	it
11.	stripe	strip	trip	trips	strips	(stripe)
12.	red	(red)	dear	read	bed	wed
13.	parents	people	parent	person	purpose	(parents)
14.	only	once	(only)	alone	lonely	one
15.	none	noisy	know	(none)	some	nose
16.	most	(most)	storm	mist	must	mast
17.	lived	lives	living	liver	loved	(lived)
18.	was	wash	saw	(was)	worst	west
19.	write	written	wrote	writing	writes	(write)
20.	early	ears	earth	(early)	eastern	curly
21.	could	couldn't	can't	pound	called	could
22.	about	apron	about	bother	another	among
23.	reply	really	reply	replied	repay	response
24.	slow	lower	slow	slower	slowest	low
25.	they	them	this	they	they're	these

STOP. Do NOT turn the page.

4 twelve lines

Exercise 20. Timed Reading

A

1   The flag of the United States has thirteen stripes. Seven are red; the others are
2   white. The blue box in the upper left-hand corner of the flag contains 50 white stars. There
3   is one star for each of the states.

4   An early flag had thirteen stripes and thirteen stars. The stripes were the same as on
5   today's flag. The blue box, however, had only thirteen stars because there were only
6   thirteen states at first.

7   The first flag was chosen on June 14, 1777, by the Continental Congress.
8   However, no one knows for sure who made the first flag. Francis Hopkinson said that he
9   had designed the first flag. In 1870, William Canby said that his grandmother, Betsy
10   Ross, had made the first American flag. We do not know if either is true.

11   Why were red, white, and blue chosen? Unfortunately, the Continental Congress
12   did not leave any record to show why these were selected.

1. The main idea of paragraph 3 (lines 7–10) is
     (A.) we do not know who made the first flag
     B. the Continental Congress made the first flag
     C. many people believe that Betsy Ross made the first flag

tampoco

2. The word *either* in line 10 means
     (A.) one of two
     B. all of them
     C. both

3. The reading does not say it, but we can guess that if the United States had only 25 states, then
     (A.) the number of stars on the flag would be different from the flag now
     B. the flag would have a blue box with 13 red stripes and 12 white stripes
     C. the colors of the flag would not be red, white, and blue

4. We know for certain that Betsy Ross
     (A) was Canby's grandmother
     B. made the first American flag
     C. was the first American to see the new flag

5. The reason that the colors red, white, and blue were used in the American flag is
     A. these three colors are very strong
     B. Betsy Ross liked these colors
     (C.) not given in this reading passage

STOP. Do NOT turn the page.

Exercise 21. Timed Word Selection

Directions: Read the word to the left of the line. Then read the five words to the right. Circle the word that is exactly the same as the word to the left of the line.

1.	about	after	although	anyone	artist	**(about)**
2.	for	form	four	**(for)**	from	fur
3.	case	care	**(case)**	cares	cases	cures
4.	stolen	steal	stronger	spoken	token	**(stolen)**
5.	art	**(art)**	tar	rat	are	ear
6.	died	dead	dies	tied	**(died)**	fried
7.	groups	group	ground	**(groups)**	green	grains
8.	liked	likes	**(liked)**	looks	looked	lucky
9.	plays	played	tray	trays	play	**(plays)**
10.	rare	**(rare)**	are	real	meat	near
11.	books	**(books)**	book	good	hooks	hook
12.	home	time	**(home)**	house	honest	phone
13.	every	**(every)**	very	everyone	everything	earth
14.	with	wish	**(with)**	west	wind	white
15.	stripes	trips	strips	trip	stripe	**(stripes)**
16.	she	he's	she's	free	**(she)**	her
17.	flag	flow	**(flag)**	flows	flags	flying
18.	career	careers	cancer	**(career)**	callers	caller
19.	call	cell	**(call)**	cold	called	elbow
20.	author	artist	**(author)**	authors	artists	earlier
21.	model	modern	money	**(model)**	label	noodle
22.	young	yearly	younger	youngest	yesterday	**(young)**
23.	very	very	every	vary	weary	early
24.	eggs	legs	begs	goes	egg	eggs
25.	born	barn	burn	brown	town	born

STOP. Do NOT turn the page.

Exercise 22. Timed Reading

1   Lou Gehrig was a very famous baseball player. In fact, he was one of the greatest
2   players of all time. Between 1925 and 1929, Gehrig played 2,130 consecutive games for
3   the New York Yankees.

4   Henry Louis Gehrig was born in New York City. He played for the same team
5   during his entire baseball career, which began in 1923. That team was the New York
6   Yankees. He played first base. Although Gehrig played extremely well, he was not as
7   famous as his teammate Babe Ruth. In 1927, Lou Gehrig hit 47 home runs, an
8   outstanding number for one year. However, Babe Ruth hit 60 home runs in the same year.

9   Gehrig retired from baseball in 1939. He had a very serious disease. The scientific
10 name for this disease is amyotrophic lateral sclerosis, a rare nerve disease that has no cure.
11 Nowadays people often call this disease Lou Gehrig's disease. He died two years later.

1. The main idea of paragraph 3 (lines 9–11) is
    A. Gehrig died from a rare disease
    B. the name of the disease that killed Gehrig is sclerosis
    C. baseball caused Gehrig to have this rare disease

2. The word *outstanding* in line 8 means
    A. outside
    B. excellent
    C. difficult

3. The reading does not say it, but we can guess that
    A. Gehrig played in every game for his team in 1927
    B. Gehrig wanted to play for three teams in 1922
    C. Gehrig never traveled outside New York City

4. This famous player died in
    A. 1939
    B. 1940
    C. 1941

5. Gehrig
    A. began and ended his career on different teams
    B. played on one team his whole career
    C. lived in the United States but never joined any team

STOP. Do NOT turn the page.

Exercise 23. Vocabulary Recall

Read the vocabulary word in boldface print on the left. Read the three choices and choose the one that is similar in meaning or has something in common with the first word. Write the letter of the answer on the line.

	Word	A	B	C
A	1. **bone**	body	use	know
B	2. **cheat**	maps	wrong	wings
B	3. **team**	time	group	without
B	4. **kick**	mouth	foot	arm
A	5. **vertical**	up-down	on-off	left-right
___	6. **donate**	give	write	purpose
___	7. **enemy**	all	friend	food
___	8. **flock**	books	big test	group
A	9. **age**	how old	how many	how long
___	10. **proper**	clean	correct	mine
___	11. **stripe**	live	lie	line
___	12. **contain**	vary	have	talk
___	13. **star**	begin	sky	post office
___	14. **fortunate**	every day	no money	lucky
___	15. **consecutive**	one-six-five	Mon-Tues-Wed	red-blue-yellow
___	16. **extremely**	sometimes	very	one more
___	17. **rare**	back	chair	unique
___	18. **retire**	young	work	bank
___	19. **hurry**	fast	river	weather
___	20. **survive**	play	live	ask
___	21. **entire**	all	feeling	find out
___	22. **mammal**	first name	no meat	warm blood
___	23. **disease**	sick	always	price
___	24. **patch**	number of times	color	area
___	25. **reply**	pay again	answer	study

Explanation for Exercise 1, p. 33:

1. museum, gallery (These are two possible places where we see famous paintings.)
2. purse (Women usually keep their money and credit cards in their purses.)
3. hurry, run (These words describe what you must do so you will not be late and you will not miss the plane.)
4. alarm (Alarm matches the description in this sentence.)
5. president (Washington, Carter, Bush, and Clinton were all presidents of the United States.)
6. sand (The only white thing at a beach is sand.)
7. library (The best answer is library. Bookstore is possible, but the description sounds more like a public library.)
8. narrow, small, little, tiny (Narrow is the best answer. It means the bridge is not wide enough for today's larger cars.)
9. free (Free means we don't have to pay anything.)
10. bones (It is a fact that we have 206 bones in our bodies. It is true that we need them to sit up or to stand up.)

Lesson 4

Extended Reading Fluency Practices

Exercise 1. Nonprose: U.S. Presidents

Use the information in this chart to answer the questions below.

President	Order	Born	Died	Years in Office
Dwight Eisenhower	34th	1890	1969	1953–61
James Garfield	20th	1831	1881	1881
Thomas Jefferson	3rd	1743	1826	1801–9
Lyndon Johnson	36th	1908	1973	1963–69
John Kennedy	35th	1917	1963	1961–63
Abraham Lincoln	16th	1809	1865	1861–65
James Madison	4th	1751	1836	1809–17
Franklin Roosevelt	32nd	1882	1945	1933–45
Theodore Roosevelt	26th	1858	1919	1901–9
Zachary Taylor	12th	1784	1850	1849–50
John Tyler	10th	1790	1862	1841–45
George Washington	1st	1732	1799	1789–97

1. The American Civil War began in 1861. Who was president when the Civil War began?

   Abraham Lincoln

2. How many presidents are on this list? ___12___

3. The usual number of years in office for a president is four or eight. Which presidents did not finish at least four years?

   James Garfield, John Kennedy,
   Zachary Taylor!

4. James Monroe was the fifth U.S. president. He was president from 1817 to 1825. He was born in 1758 and died in 1831. Add this information to the correct place in the chart. (Hint: How are the names

   listed on this chart? Is there a special method?) _between Madison and_

   Roosevelt

5. Who was born first—Tyler, Monroe, or Taylor? ___Monroe___

6. Who was the first U.S. president? _Gorge Washington_

7. John Kennedy was assassinated in 1963. Who became president after he was killed?
Johnson

8. Which presidents were born in the 1700s (the 18th century)? _Jefferson_

_____

9. Can you think of the names of any U.S. presidents whose names are not on this list? _____
Clinton, Bush, Carter _____

10. Do you know anything about the presidents on this list? _____

_____

Which names have you heard before and which are new to you? _Dwingh Eisenhower,_
Zachary Taylor, John Tyler. _____

Exercise 2. Nonfiction: Giraffes

Part 1. Prereading. What do you know about giraffes? Answer these questions. If you do not know, guess.

1. Which is taller: a male giraffe or a female giraffe? _male_

2. In meters or feet, what is the average height of a male giraffe? _17 feet or_

3. Giraffes have longer necks than humans, but humans have the same number of bones in their

   necks. <u>TRUE</u> FALSE

4. Giraffes usually sleep lying on top of grass. TRUE <u>FALSE</u>

5. A baby giraffe is about 3 feet tall (1 meter) at birth. TRUE <u>FALSE</u>

6. Giraffes spend most of their life in only two areas. TRUE <u>FALSE</u>

7. Giraffes can close their noses completely to keep out sand and dust. <u>TRUE</u> FALSE

8. The food that giraffes usually eat is grass. <u>TRUE</u> FALSE

9. A baby giraffe begins to walk when it is only one week old. TRUE <u>FALSE</u>

10. Giraffes protect themselves with their teeth, legs, and feet. TRUE FALSE

's with a partner. When you have finished, read the passage on giraffes.
ircle your answers that are correct and put an X on your answers that are

Giraffes

lest animal that is alive today. The average height for a male giraffe is about
e the average height for a female giraffe is about 14 feet (4.3 meters). Almost
t comes from its long legs and long neck.

The g...   teresting animal because it has a unique body. The giraffe's body has light
brown or light yellow patches on it. These patches make the giraffe's body blend in with the trees and
this coloring helps protect the giraffe. The giraffe can
close both its nostrils completely to keep out dust and sand.
The giraffe uses its long upper lip and its tongue to grab
food (mostly leaves) from high tree branches. Although
it has an extremely long neck, there are only seven bones
in it—which is the same number of bones that most mam-
mals, including humans, have in their necks. When giraffes walk, they move both right legs and then both left
legs. When they run, they move both back legs to the
front and then both front legs to the front. Giraffes can
run very quickly—up to 35 miles per hour. Giraffes usually sleep standing up. In order to drink water, giraffes
must spread apart their front legs and then bend down so they can reach the water.

Giraffe

A female can have her first calf (the term for young giraffes) when she is about five years old. A
female giraffe is pregnant for about 15 months. A calf can be 6 feet tall at birth and can walk an hour
after birth.

In their natural habitat, giraffes can live up to 28 years. Giraffes spend most of their entire life in
a small area. This area is usually about 29 square miles (75 square kilometers). Females and their
young often stay in small groups.

Giraffes protect themselves by using their strong legs and feet. The only natural enemy of an
adult giraffe is a lion. Sometimes a giraffe is able to kill a lion by kicking it. Another enemy of the
giraffe, unfortunately, is man. People have hunted giraffes and people have taken land for farms and
forced the giraffes to leave the area.

There are now ranches where giraffes are raised for their meat. Some experts think that this is
good because many Africans do not eat enough meat, and giraffe meat could help their diet. Giraffes
are also a better source of meat than cows or sheep because giraffes can survive better on the kinds of
tropical plants found in Africa than cows or sheep can.

STRATEGY 6:
New Words: Skip Them

**Skip a word that is very difficult to guess. If you
find a new word, first try to guess its meaning. If
you cannot guess the meaning, skip it! Forget this
word and continue reading the other sentences.
Sometimes skipping the word is OK.**

Part 3.   Outline of the reading. Fill in the missing numbers and words to complete the outline for the reading. Use the words below.

color	~~protection~~	14 feet tall	~~enemies~~
~~dust~~	lips	~~legs~~	~~pregnant~~
~~baby giraffes~~	bones	diet	~~place~~

I. Tallest animal
    A. Male: 17 feet tall
    B. Female: _14 feet tall_

II. Unique
    A. _Color_ : protection
    B. Nose: keep out _dust_ and sand
    C. _lips_ and tongue: reach food
    D. Long neck: number of _bones_ same as human neck
    E. _legs_ : can run quickly
    F. Sleep: standing up

III. _Baby Giraffes_
    A. Mother:
        1. First calf when mother is 5 years old (possible)
        2. _Pregnant_ for 15 months
    B. Baby:
        1. Can be 6 feet tall when born
        2. Can walk when 1 hour old

IV. Life
    A. Age: up to 28 years old
    B. _place_ : entire life in small area (29 square miles)
    C. Group: females and young stay in groups

V. _Protection_
    A. Weapons: legs and feet
    B. _Enemies_ : lions and men

VI. Ranches
    A. Giraffe meat: good for African _diet_
    B. Other animals: giraffes can live better in Africa than cows or sheep

Exercise 3. Fiction

Part 1. This story is a mystery. Read about the crime and then decide who the guilty person is. Answer the questions in the boxes. Good luck!

The Case of the Stolen Painting (826 words)

Questions: 1. What do you think this story is about?

2. Where do you think this story takes place?

Museum, Galery, Collection's house

"Could you tell me what happened?" asked Officer Underhill.

It was just 7:45 in the morning, and Officer Underhill was already at the Norwood City Art Museum. The director of the museum, Adam Nix, was explaining the theft of one of the museum's most valuable paintings to Officer Underhill.

Questions: 3. Where are they? *Inside Musaum*

4. Why are they there?

Becaus is a robery

"Well, I got here around 7:15 and found the back door open. It was strange because I am always the first person here, and I'm the one who usually opens all the doors here in the morning."

"Was the lock on the door broken?" asked Officer Underhill. A few other officers were walking around now, looking for any clues that might help them to catch the thief.

"No," replied Mr. Nix, "it wasn't. The door was open and I walked in and looked around. That's when I saw it."

"Saw what?" Officer Underhill asked Mr. Nix. "What did you see?"

"A painting was missing from the east wall in the modern art room. *Roses by the Window* was our most valuable painting. It cost us more than half a million dollars!"

Officer Underhill continued with his questions. "What about the alarm? Didn't the alarm go off?"

"No, it didn't," said Mr. Nix. "I don't know why it didn't go off."

> Question 5.: The alarm didn't go off. Is this strange? Why or why not?
> *Yes, because somevary didn't go off.*

"Mr. Nix, who had keys to the museum?"

"Well, of course I had a set of keys. Then Mr. Potts and Mrs. Jackson have a set."

"Who are they?" asked the officer.

"Mr. Potts is my assistant, and Mrs. Jackson is our head secretary." Mr. Nix continued, "They've both worked here for as long as I can remember."

Just then Mr. Potts walked into the museum. It was 7:55.

"Mr. Nix, what happened?" asked the newcomer.

"I'm afraid we've had a robbery during the night. One of the —"

Just then the officer interrupted. "Good morning, sir. My name is Officer Underhill and I'm here to investigate the theft of the painting. What can you tell me about it?"

"Well, I don't know much about that painting. It's new to the museum," said Mr. Potts.

"That's right," added Mr. Nix. "We just got *Roses by the Window* about three weeks ago."

Officer Underhill spoke again. "What do you know about this painting?"

"Well, as Mr. Nix said, we got it about three weeks ago. And I know that it was very, very expensive. Some of the museum directors didn't think it was good to buy such an expensive painting, but they decided to buy it anyway."

"Mr. Potts, where were you last night?" asked the police officer.

"Well, I was home all night," answered the man.

"Was anyone with you?" continued Officer Underhill.

Mr. Potts thought for a minute. "No," he began, "I'm single, and I was alone last night."

Just then a woman came into the museum. "Oh, Mr. Nix, I'm sorry to be late again, but —" Just then she saw the policeman and her voice stopped. With a very surprised look on her face, she continued talking. "What is going on here?"

> Question 6.: Who do you think she is?
> *Next parson*

Mr. Nix began explaining. "There was a robbery last night or early this morning. Someone took our *Roses by the Window*." There was an empty look on the woman's face. "And this is Officer Underhill," said Mr. Nix as he turned toward the officer. "He's investigating the case."

"Good morning," said Officer Underhill. "You must be Mrs. Jackson. I'm Officer Underhill and I'm in charge of this case."

"Yes, I see," she said, still in shock over the theft of the painting.

"Mr. Nix told me that you have a set of keys to the museum. Do you still have your keys?" asked the officer.

"Yes, I do," she said rather quietly. "They're right here in my purse," she said as she put her left hand in her purse. She pulled out a set of shiny keys and said, "Yes, here they are."

Turning to Mr. Potts, the officer said, "What about you, Mr. Potts? Do you still have a set of keys to the museum?"

"Sure. I have always had a set of keys to this museum," answered Mr. Potts.

The two police officers who had been looking around in the modern art room walked into the room where the four people were standing. One of them turned toward the officer and said, "We're finished, sir. We're ready to go back to the office to think about this crime."

"OK, everyone, I'm going back to my office now. Just as soon as I know something, I'll call you," said Officer Underhill.

"Well, thank you very much for coming out so quickly. We'll clean up the area around where the missing painting was. We have to hurry because we open at 9 A.M. That only gives us about 25 more minutes," announced Mr. Nix.

Question 7.: What time is it right now? 7:35

Later that afternoon, Officer Underhill called up Mr. Nix. "Mr. Nix, this is Officer Underhill. We

believe that we know who stole the painting. The name of the thief is *ladron* _Mr. Potts_ ."

What is the name that Officer Underhill told Mr. Nix? _____

Why did Officer Underhill believe that this person was the thief? _____

_____

_____

_____

_____

Part 2.   Discuss your answers to the questions in part 1 with a partner or with your class and teacher.

Part 3.   Summary Practice. Read this summary of the minimystery. The minimystery has 826 words, but this summary has only 164 words. Some of the words are missing. Fill in the blanks with a correct word.

Summary of "The Case of the Stolen Painting"

There was a theft at the Norwood City Art Museum, so the director, Mr. Nix, (1)_____*called*_____

the police. Officer Underhill went to the museum to find out what happened. Mr. Nix explained that the

(2)_____*back*_____ door was open when he arrived at 7:15. The (3)_____*lock*_____ was not broken. Mr.

Nix went into the museum and saw that *Roses by the Window,* a new (4)_____*painting*_____ that the museum

had paid half a million dollars for, was missing. As they (5)_____*were*_____ talking, Mr. Potts, who

worked at the museum , arrived at 7:55. Officer Underhill explained what had happened. A little later, Mrs.

Jackson, another employee of the (6)_____*museum*_____ , arrived. Mr. Nix explained what had happened during the night. Officer Underhill asked both employees if they had their (7)___Keys___ . Both Mr.

Potts and Mrs. (8)___Jackson___ said that they still had their keys. Officer Underhill (9)___left___

at about 8:35. Later in the day, Officer Underhill called Mr. Nix (10)___and___ said that he knew

who had stolen the painting.

Exercise 4. News Reports: True or False?

Read these three news stories. Two of them are false and one of them is true. Circle true or false. Then answer the question at the end of this exercise.

1. true or <u>false?</u>   **Winning Record for High School Team**

Basketball is a very popular sport in the United States. It is a very important sport at many high schools. A high school in Miami, Florida, recently set a national record for the most consecutive wins by a high school basketball team. The most recent win gave the school a record of 160 wins without a single loss. This year the team finished with a perfect 32–0 record. Two games were close, as the team won by a margin of only one point (80–79 and 64–63), but many of the other wins were by margins of more than 25 points.

2. true or false?   **Rare Animals Found in New York House**

In Syracuse, New York, police were surprised when they went to the home of Vincent Pace. The police found 74 animals inside the house. These animals included an African lion, an Indian tiger, and an Australian wallaby. The police were called to come because many of the animals were protected animals. It is against the law for people to own these animals. Pace said that he had done nothing wrong. He said that he took care of the animals, that the animals were in good shape, and that he gave them to new owners.

3. true or <u>false?</u>   **A Big Car Sale**

In Los Angeles, California, there was a super sale of cars recently. The car dealership was 40 years old, so they had a big birthday celebration for the company. There was a birthday cake and some small joke gifts for some of the salespeople. However, the big news was the present for 100 lucky customers. Everyone wrote his or her phone number on a small card, and Leon Jamison, the owner of the car dealership, pulled 100 cards from a big box. These 100 people were able to buy any car, even the brand-new cars, for only $40 (forty dollars) each! This was such a big sale that over 8,000 people came to the dealership location to write their name on a card. They all wanted a chance to buy a car for such a low, low price.

I think number ___2___ is true because ___Some this animals are___ ___in extintion and some people like have___

_____

_____

_____

Exercise 5. Reading/Discussion/Writing: Cheating on a Test at School

Part 1.   Read this letter from a person who has a problem with a test at school. Then work with a classmate to discuss your answers to the questions after the letter.

> *Dear Advisor,*
>
>   *I've got a problem about something at school. I hope you can give me some good advice about what to do.*
>
>   *I'm a senior in high school, and it's time for the final exams. My worst subject is history, and of course I am worried about the final exam in this class. My best friend Theo bought a copy of the final exam. I don't know how he did this or who he got it from, but I am sure that he has a copy of the test.*
>
>   *Theo is my good friend. He told me that he will give me a copy of the test if I want one. I don't know what to do. I know that this is cheating, and I know that cheating is wrong. However, a lot of people in my class will see the copy of the test, so I might be the only person who does not look at it. I am worried about my grade in this class. History is my worst subject.*
>
>   *What should I do? Should I do what everyone else is doing? Or should I just study without looking at Theo's copy of the test? I don't want my friends to laugh at me for being so stupid.*
>
> *Kirk*

Part 2.   Discuss your answers to these questions with a classmate.

1. What is Kirk's problem?
2. What do you think he should do?
3. If you were the teacher and you found that Theo had a copy of the test, what would you do?
4. Have you ever cheated on a test? What was the situation? Did the teacher catch you? If yes, what happened?

Part 3.   Now read these responses from four different people. Which response do you think is the best? *№ 3*
Why? Which one is the worst? Why do you think this?

Answer 1

Dear Kirk,

This is an easy letter for me to write. Don't be stupid. Your friend Theo has a copy of the test. You are not a good history student. Of course you have to look at the test.

It's important not to make a perfect 100 score on the test. Be sure to miss three or four of the questions. You don't want the teacher to find out what happened. You are not a good student in history class, so if you suddenly make a very high score, the teacher will definitely be suspicious.

Belinda

Answer 2

Dear Kirk,

You are writing this letter because you know in your heart that this is wrong. Do what your heart tells you to do. I think your heart is telling you that this is wrong and that you should not do this.

Your friend Theo has done something very, very wrong. If you look at the test, then this is only making the problem bigger. Stop now.

I also think that you have to tell the teacher that Theo has a copy of the test. If you do not say anything to the teacher, then this is a form of lying. You have to tell the complete truth, 100% of the truth. Talk to the teacher. If you don't want to do this, maybe you can write a letter to the teacher without signing your name on it.

Steven

Answer 3

Dear Kirk,

Don't look at the test. You have to study from your book. Whether your grade is good or bad is not important. It will be your grade. Your test should be what you really know.

Study as much as you can. Don't worry what Theo and your friends say. If they are really your friends, then they will understand your thinking in this situation.

Good luck!

Paul

Answer 4

Dear Kirk,

History is not your good subject. Theo is your best friend. Theo has the history test. Theo wants to give you a copy of the test. What is the problem? I think today is your lucky, lucky day! This is not bad. If something is bad, then someone is getting hurt. However, no one is getting hurt.

I want to say "Good luck on your history test!" but this is not necessary. Of course you will do well on your history test. Don't forget to say thanks to your good friend Theo.

Melissa

Part 4. For homework, write your own reply letter to Kirk. Follow the four examples in part 3. Write your own opinion. Try to limit your answer to 125 words. Be sure to say EXACTLY what you think Kirk should do. Be sure to give reasons why Kirk should follow your suggestion.

At the next class, pass around your papers so that everyone gets to read everyone else's letters.

STRATEGY 7:
New Words: Use the Dictionary

If you can't guess the meaning of a new word and if you can't skip it, then look up the word in your dictionary. Try to guess the meaning of the word. If you can't guess the meaning, skip the word. If you can't understand the idea of the group of sentences without knowing the meaning of that word, then it's OK to look it up in your dictionary. But first try to guess or to skip it!

Lesson 5

Exercises and Skills Practices

Exercise 1. Context Clues: Logical Groupings

Complete each sentence with your own words. Then discuss your answers with a partner or with your class. There may be no single best answer at times. Possible answers are on page 89.

1. Carrots, broccoli, spinach, and other _vegetables_ are very important for good health.

2. I think the best choices for a car are red, blue, or _white_ .

3. Most children like to see the monkeys, the lions, and the _elephant_ when they go to the zoo.

4. In our home aquarium, we have _fish_ , snails, and plants.

5. Helen likes all kinds of desserts. She likes cake, cookies, and _pie._ _Ice cream_ .

6. Some of the largest whales can be found in the Arctic, the Pacific, and the _Atlantic Ocean_

7. The best times to plant those flowers are March, _April_ , or May.

8. I was always good at math, science, English, and _history_ , but I never liked geography class.

9. Questions number one, two, and _three_ were not so difficult, but number four through number ten were too hard for me.

10. A triangle, a _square_ , and a rectangle are easy to draw if you have a ruler, but a ruler won't help you draw a circle.

11. Chocolate, vanilla, and _strawberry_ are good flavors for ice cream.

12. To cook beans, you really only need beans, salt, and _water_ , but some people like to add a little meat.

carrots

aquarium

whale

Exercise 2. Context Clues

In each of these sentences, you will find an italicized word or group of words. Read the three choices and then decide which choice means about the same as the italicized word or words. Circle the letter of your answer.

1. No one knows how many people were at the meeting, but *approximately* sixty people were there.
   A. sometimes
   B. many
   C. about

2. My father told me, "Don't quit your job. Keep working at the bank for one more year. If you are not happy then, look for a new job." This was very good *advice*.
   A. news
   B. suggestion
   C. work

3. Doctor Madison told Mr. Jones to *cut down on* coffee. A little coffee was OK, but Mr. Jones shouldn't drink as much as he is drinking now.
   A. stop drinking
   B. drink less
   C. drink tea or cola (in place of coffee)

4. There is only a *slight* difference between these two dictionaries. Either of them is a good choice for foreign students who are studying English.
   A. small
   B. outstanding
   C. important

5. An *island* is a body of land that has water on all sides.
   A. the United States
   B. Florida
   C. Hawaii

6. It was difficult to *come up with* an answer for this question.
   A. make, produce
   B. send, give
   C. change, erase

STRATEGY 8: Titles

Look at the title of the reading before you begin. If there is a title, read this quickly. You can usually get some idea of what a reading is about by looking at the title of a reading. For example, look at the title on page 109. What do you think the reading is about? Try this strategy with your reading in the future.

Exercise 3. Context Clues + Dictionary Work

In each of these sentences, you will find an italicized word or group of words. Read the sentence and then write your guess about the meaning of the word. Then look up the word in a dictionary and write the real meaning.

1. If your business is _successful_, you will be rich and many people will know your name.

   YOUR GUESS: _____

   REAL MEANING: _Victory, better a lot all money._
   Make money

2. She studied French in high school. _In addition_, she studied Spanish and Japanese.

   YOUR GUESS: _____

   REAL MEANING: _Also,_

3. He said the train will arrive around 4:30, but the _precise_ arrival time is 4:32.

   YOUR GUESS: _____

   REAL MEANING: _definitue, exactly, on time_

4. I didn't like that restaurant very much. The waitress was very _rude_ to me. She wasn't very nice to us and she didn't tell us thank you or anything when we left.

   YOUR GUESS: _____

   REAL MEANING: _discourteous, respect, dignity_

5. An island is a body of land that is _surrounded_ by water.
   alrededor

   YOUR GUESS: _____

   REAL MEANING: _circuly, All sides,_

6. The Vietnam _Memorial_ in Washington, D.C., has the names of all the American soldiers who died in the Vietnam War.

   YOUR GUESS: _____

   REAL MEANING: _Remembery, Monument tribute_

   Vietnam Veterans Memorial USA 20c

7. Emily bought a new radio. After two days, it broke. She took it back to the store and got her money back. This was _logical_. Ken bought a new TV. After one week, it broke. He threw it in the garbage and bought another new TV. This was not _logical_.

   YOUR GUESS: _____

   REAL MEANING: _Consecuences, commonsense make sense._

8. *Instead of* eating candy, you should eat fresh fruits and vegetables.

     YOUR GUESS: _____

     REAL MEANING: *better option, in place of, subtitud, alternative*

9. The bill at the restaurant was $20, and I left $3 for the *tip*. The total was $23.

     YOUR GUESS: _____

     REAL MEANING: *gift, bonus, reward*

10. I have English class on Monday and Wednesday only, but my math class meets *daily*.

     YOUR GUESS: _____

     REAL MEANING: *every day,*

11. Should I go to the University of South Florida or should I go to North Texas University? I don't know what to do. This is a very difficult *decision* for me.

     YOUR GUESS: _____

     REAL MEANING: *decide, answer, result, choose make up the mind*

12. We now live in a small house on Fig Street. Our *previous* house was on Madison Street.

     YOUR GUESS: _____

     REAL MEANING: *before, former*

13. The doctor said that the pain in my arm is not in the skin. It is an *internal* problem.

     YOUR GUESS: _____

     REAL MEANING: *inside,*

14. He dropped a ball into the water, but the water was moving so *swiftly* that the ball was gone in a few seconds.

     YOUR GUESS: _____

     REAL MEANING: *fast, rapid, quickly*

15. Some people are afraid to go into that old house because they think there are *ghosts* there from people who lived there over 200 years ago.

     YOUR GUESS: _____

     REAL MEANING: *spirits,*

este   ese aquestos aquellos

Exercise 4. Language Focus: Markers *this, that, these, those*

1. with the same noun

   Many people live in my building. These people work at the bank and the store.
   (these people = the people in my building)

   Here is a picture of my house. This picture was taken two months ago.
   (this picture = the picture of my house)

2. with a different noun (synonym)

   The president has proposed a new plan. This idea will help the country.
   (this idea = the president's new plan)

   White wrote *Grapes of India* in 1931. This book discusses work problems.
   (this book = *Grapes of India*)

3. by itself (no noun)

   He likes to eat chicken curry. This is a common food in Malaysia.
   (this = chicken curry)

   She visited Miami in 1991. That was her favorite place.
   (that = Miami)

Underline the correct word. Draw an arrow to what your answer refers to. Follow the first example.

example: I like iced tea very much. [This, These] drink is very good when the weather is very hot.

Topic: the state of South Dakota, Numbers 1–3

1. South Dakota is in the northern part of the United States. The capital of [this, these] state is Pierre, but

   [this, these] city is not the largest city.

2. Thousands of people visit South Dakota every year. [This, These] people come to see Mount Rushmore

   National Memorial in the southwestern part of [this, these] state.

3. In 1876, the Homestake Gold Mine was opened. [This, These] is the oldest continuous gold mine in

   the world. Millions of tons of [this, these] valuable metal have come out of this mine.

Topic: the Statue of Liberty, Numbers 4–6

4. The Statue of Liberty is a symbol of the United States. It
    is located in New York. More than two million tourists
    visit [this, these] famous site every year.

5. Where do [this, these] people come from? They come
    from countries all over the world.

6. Do you know the story of how, when, and why [this, these]
    famous attraction came to the United States? [This, These]
    is really an amazing story. The answers to [this, these]
    questions are very interesting.

Exercise 5. Language Focus: Markers *this, that, these, those*

1. Circle this, that, these, or those. If there is a noun, circle the noun also.

    example: I like (this.) OR (This answer) is correct.

2. On the line, write what the circled word means.

    example: I like blue. (This color) is my favorite.   _____blue_____

Topic: the state of Delaware, Numbers 1–3

1. Delaware is a very small state in the northeastern part of the United
    States. Henry Hudson came to this area in 1609.   *this area*

2. Some of the largest companies in the United States have their offices in
    Delaware. A good example of one of these is Du Pont, which is one of
    the world's largest chemical companies.   *this larget*
                                                                               company

3. The tax laws in this state are very good for   *this slate*

    these companies, so they have set up their businesses in Delaware.   *these companies*

Topic: the sinking of the *Titanic*, Numbers 4–5

4.   On April 14, 1912, the *Titanic* hit an iceberg (a large piece of ice) in the
     Atlantic Ocean. The ship sank. Many people died. The precise number
     of people who died in this accident isn't known, but more than one

     thousand people lost their lives that night.

     this maiden
     that night

5.   This news shocked the world. Most people thought

     this was impossible because the *Titanic* was such a large ship.

     this news
     This was

Topic: a new medical report about eating fish, Numbers 6–9

6.   Some people eat a lot of fish. They do this because they think if eating
     a little fish is good, then eating a lot of fish is very good for us.

     This eat fish

7.   For many years, doctors told us eating fish is very good for our health.
     Doctors said eating fish is good because it helps to stop heart disease.
     However, a recent study does not agree with this previous advice.

     This advice

8.   Dr. Alberto Ascherio, who is the main author of this recent report, said
     eating fish is not bad for us. "But some people may be eating fish
     instead of eating vegetables or exercising." This is not good.

     This report
     _____

9.   So will people stop eating so much fish because of this report?

     That is an interesting question, but most people think it will not change
     people's eating habits.

     this report
     that is an
     interesting

STRATEGY 9: Past Tense

Pay attention to past tense markers. Sometimes a
reading will have many past tense markers.
Examples are *-ed* (wanted, died, believed),
yesterday, last month, and five years ago. These
markers tell us that the topic of the reading is
something that has happened already. For
example, a reading about history uses many past
tense markers. Why is this?

Exercise 6. Sentence Study: Details

Read these sentences carefully. Read the question and then circle the letter of the correct answer.

1. The *Titanic,* which was a very large ship made in Britain, was so big and strong that most people thought that nothing could ever happen to it.

   Which of these is not true?
      A. It was made in Britain.
      B. It was an airplane.
      C. It was extremely big.
      D. People believed it was very safe.

2. Alexander Graham Bell was born in Edinburgh, Scotland, in 1847, but he and his family went to Canada in 1870.

   What happened in 1847?
      A. Bell moved to Scotland.
      B. Bell moved to Canada with his family.
      C. Bell's family left Scotland.
      D. Bell was born.

3. A turkey sandwich is $2.50, a cheeseburger is $2.25, a soft drink is $1.25, and fries are $1.10, but you can get either sandwich, a soft drink, and fries for $4.25.

   Which of these is cheapest?
      A. a turkey sandwich, a soft drink, and fries
      B. a cheeseburger, a soft drink, and fries
      C. a turkey sandwich and fries
      D. a cheeseburger and a soft drink

4. The Statue of Liberty, a famous tourist attraction located in New York City, was given to the United States by the people of France in 1884 as a sign of friendship.

   Who gave the Statue of Liberty to whom?
      A. France gave it to the United States.
      B. The United States gave it to France.
      C. France gave it to New York City.
      D. New York City gave it to France.

Exercise 7. Sentence Study: Conclusions

Read these sentences carefully. Read the four choices and then circle t⟨...⟩ think is true from the information in the sentences.

1. Alexander Graham Bell worked with an American inventor to ⟨...⟩ dian inventor to develop a hydrofoil.
   A. Bell was American.
   B. Bell invented more than one thing.
   C. The airplane was an international invention.
   D. The Canadian inventor was richer than the American inventor.

2. A cheeseburger is $1.50, a soft drink is 90 cents, and french fries are 60 cents, but you can get a cheeseburger set that includes all three of these for only $2.50.
   A. The cheeseburger set is cheaper.
   B. The fries are more expensive if you get a hamburger.
   C. It's better to get two soft drinks.
   D. The cheeseburger set includes a large soft drink.

3. The man tried to find his axe in the river. He looked and looked, but the water was moving so swiftly that he couldn't see his axe anywhere.
   A. The man does not have the axe now.
   B. The water is in a large glass.
   C. The man was blind.
   D. The man is not near a river.

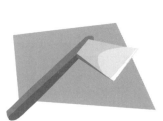

4. Doctors agree that eating dark, leafy vegetables such as broccoli and cabbage is good for your health.
   A. So eating spinach is probably good for your health.
   B. So doctors prefer broccoli more than cabbage.
   C. So dark leafy vegetables are the most important food for your good health.
   D. So doctors don't know how much broccoli is good for you.

Exercise 8. Main Idea

There are two paragraphs in this exercise. Read each paragraph quickly to discover the author's main idea. Read the four possible answers and circle the letter of the one that you think is the main idea. Remember that the main idea is the idea that the whole or complete paragraph discusses.

1. Some people eat a lot of fish. They do this because they think that eating a little fish is good, so then eating a lot of fish is very good for us. Dr. Martijn Katan, a doctor in the Netherlands, said that perhaps this is not 100% true. A little fish may be good for us, but the doctor said that this does not mean that a lot of fish is very good for us.

   A. Eating fish is not so good for people.
   B. Is fish good for us? There are two ideas about this.
   C. One doctor in the Netherlands thinks that this is not precisely true.
   D. We know that eating a little fish is good, so eating more is better.

ch is enough for a tip? The waiter's job is to serve you the customer. Service is his job. If his
e was not good, then you have no obligation to leave any tip. The word tip stands for "to insure
mptness." In other words, we leave a tip so the waiter will know that he is going to be paid for his
rvice. If the service is good, the tip is good. If the service is not good, then the tip is not good either.

A. A tip varies with the service.
B. A tip is something you have to give to the waiter after the meal.
C. The writer believes that leaving a tip for the waiter is logical.
D. The customer has to help the waiter's situation.

Exercise 9. Organization + Main Idea

There are two paragraphs in this exercise. In each paragraph, there is one sentence that is not related to the
main idea or topic of the paragraph. Draw a line through the sentence that does not belong in the paragraph.
Then read the four answers and circle the letter of the main idea.

1. One of the first Europeans to come to the place that we call Delaware today was Henry Hudson.
    However, we call this place Delaware, not Hudson. A year after Hudson arrived, a ship from the
    nearby colony of Virginia came to this area. This bay is not very deep. The captain of the ship named
    the water for Lord De La Warr, who was the governor of Virginia.

    A. Henry Hudson was the first European to come to Delaware.
    B. People lived in Virginia before they lived in Delaware.
    C. The captain sailed the ship from Virginia to Delaware.
    D. The origin of the name of the state of Delaware is interesting.

2. On the corner of Green Street and Jackson Avenue is Jack's Sandwich Shop. This is one of the best
    restaurants in town. People like the food here, especially the cheeseburgers. The food is good, and the
    prices are very good, too. There are seven kinds of sandwiches. These are hamburgers, cheesebur-
    gers, roast beef, tuna salad, chicken, egg salad, and turkey. Tuna salad sandwiches cost $1.75. In
    addition, you can eat side orders such as french fries, soup, and coleslaw. There are many kinds of soft
    drinks, and you can eat delicious desserts, too.

    A. Tuna salad sandwiches cost more than cheeseburgers.
    B. French fries, soup, and coleslaw are side orders.
    C. Jack's Sandwich Shop is a very popular restaurant.
    D. People like this place because there are seven kinds of sandwiches.

Exercise 10. Scanning

Read the two questions and the three answers first. Read the paragraph as quickly as possible to find the answers to the two questions. Circle the letter of your answer.

1. The man ate chicken with
   A. mushrooms
   B. salad
   C. cream sauce

2. Unlike the man, the woman thought that the waiter should receive
   A. 5%
   B. 10%
   C. 15%

    Last night my wife and I had dinner at a restaurant not far from our home. We like this place very much, and we have eaten there many times. Last night, however, the service was not very good. We had to wait a long time before a waiter came to our table. He was very nice, but he didn't do a very good job. I ordered chicken with mushrooms, but he brought me chicken with cream sauce. My wife got her main course OK, but he put the wrong kind of salad dressing on her salad. We didn't say anything to the waiter. We just ate what he brought us. I know that 15% is the usual amount for a tip. I wanted to leave 10%, but my wife said we should just leave 5% to show that we were not happy. In the end, I left 10% tip. Did I do the right thing?

STRATEGY 10: Quotation Marks

Read the information that is in quotation marks ("Hi, how are you?"). The words that are inside quotation marks are words that someone spoke. We find this kind of punctuation in conversations and dialogues. John said, "It's hot in here." A few seconds later, Mary answered, "Well, yes, it is quite hot this afternoon." (Look at page 58 for examples.)

Exercise 11. Sequencing/Prediction

There are four paragraphs in this exercise, but the paragraphs have been cut into three pieces. Read all the pieces and then draw a line to connect the three pieces that make a good paragraph. Use one piece from each column (A, B, C) to make each new paragraph.

A	**B**	**C**
1. A cat named Minnie recently gave birth to four babies. This is not strange at all.	When the water is boiling, add 2 cups of raw rice. When the water is boiling again, stir this one time.	Veterinarians (animal doctors) cannot explain how or why a dog and a cat decided to do this, but the result is very clear.
2. Thousands of people visit South Dakota every year. They go there to see Mount Rushmore National Memorial in the Black Hills.	Residents who live nearby were worried about all the noise when the people applauded. The residents wanted to stop the concert.	Put a lid on the pot and turn the fire down as low as possible. Do not lift the lid. Cook this for fourteen minutes. Serve hot with your favorite meat or vegetable dish.
3. First, you have to boil four cups of water. Add two teaspoons of salt.	This famous place has very large stone faces of four U.S. presidents. These are Washington, Jefferson, Roosevelt, and Lincoln.	The group in charge of the concert came up with a special answer to the noise problem. Their solution helped to stop the noise from the applause.
4. There was a special problem at a concert in Hong Kong. There were 17,500 people who were at this concert.	What is unusual is that the father of these babies isn't another cat but rather a dog!	These faces are extremely big! In fact, they are sixty feet high.

Exercise 12. Following Directions

Read these instructions and do what they say. Use the space below. You may want to use a pencil for this exercise so you can erase if you make a mistake. Good luck!

In the box below, draw a line from the top right corner to the bottom left corner. This will give you two triangles.

In the triangle on the right, draw a line from the bottom right corner to the opposite side of this triangle. In the new bottom triangle, print your first name in all capital letters. Draw a line under every vowel in your name.

If your birthday is in a month that has only 30 days, write the number 30 in the new triangle on the right side. If your birthday is in a month that has 31 days, write the number 100 in the new triangle on the right side. If you were born in February, write the word February in the triangle.

Then, in the other triangle, draw two circles that are equal in size and that do not touch each other. Draw one circle on top of the other. Do not draw them side by side.

In the top circle, draw an animal in a zoo that people like to see. In the bottom circle, draw a picture of your favorite fruit or vegetable.

Now write your teacher's name at the bottom of this page. Last, circle all the letters in your name that you and your teacher have in common.

Now read all the directions one more time to check your answer.

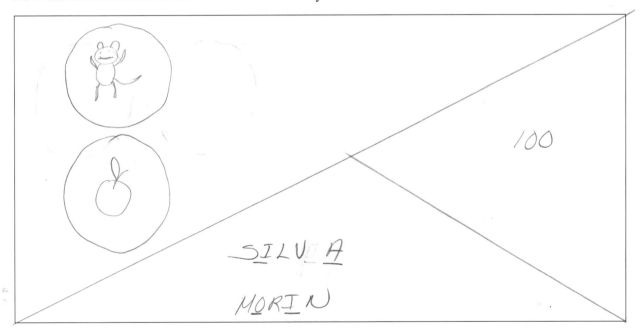

STOP. Do NOT turn the page now. WAIT for your teacher to tell you to begin work.

19

Exercise 13. Timed Word Selection

Directions: Read the word to the left of the line. Then read the five words to the right. Circle the word that is exactly the same as the word to the left of the line.

1. day	days	say	hay	(day)	says
2. boat	boats	boots	bowl	(boat)	boot
3. built	build	(built)	beetle	belts	building
4. area	are	arid	(area)	hair	ears
5. captain	capital	(captain)	capitals	captains	carpet
6. hole	older	hold	(hole)	heel	hold
7. elevators	electric	elevator	enormous	(elevators)	examples
8. icy	ice	ace	easy	lazy	(icy)
9. first	fast	fist	furs	burst	(first)
10. donated	donate	donates	(donated)	donating	donor
11. enough	every	exact	example	enormous	(enough)
12. has	had	have	he's	his	(has)
13. deaf	leaf	head	(deaf)	deal	dead
14. than	then	that	this	(than)	thin
15. states	statue	(states)	started	start	statues
16. leave	large	leaves	left	(leave)	larger
17. miles	mine	males	smile	(miles)	mile
18. married	marry	(married)	worried	worries	hurried
19. invention	inventor	invented	inventions	invent	(invention)
20. smaller	smallest	small	smiled	(smaller)	speller
21. one	only	once	one	tone	bone
22. site	sit	sat	bite	site	sitting
23. sink	sink	sank	sunk	think	sing
24. ranks	rang	rings	ranked	rank	ranks
25. oldest	old	older	coldest	boldest	oldest

STOP. Do NOT turn the page.

STRATEGY 11:
Vocabulary Notebook

Keep a vocabulary notebook! This is very important. You will learn hundreds of new words. It is not possible for you to remember all these words (or even most of them) without help. The best form of help to remember vocabulary is to write the words down in a special notebook. There is an example of this on page 133.

Exercise 14. Timed Reading

1   Delaware is a very small state in the northeastern United States. In fact, only the
2 state of Rhode Island is smaller <u>than</u> Delaware.

3   Henry Hudson came to this area in 1609. A year later, a ship from the nearby
4 colony of Virginia came into Delaware Bay. The captain named the bay for Lord De La
5 Warr, then governor of Virginia. This is how the state got its name.

6   The laws in Delaware are very good for companies, so approximately 200,000 are
7 located there. Some of the largest companies in the United States have their main offices
8 there. An example of this is Du Pont, one of the world's largest chemical companies.

9   With only 700,000 people, Delaware ranks 46th of the 50 states in population. The
10 largest city is Wilmington, a very old city, but the capital is Dover.

1. The main idea of paragraph 3 (lines 6–8) is
   A. Du Pont is a very large chemical company that is in this state
   B. many companies want to do business in this state
   C. most of the 200,000 Delaware companies make chemicals

2. The word *bay* in line 4 means
   A. an area of water
   B. an area of land
   C. an area of sand

3. The reading does not say it, but we can guess that
   A. Virginia is older than Delaware
   B. Delaware has a very large population
   C. Dover is newer and bigger than Wilmington

4. There are 50 U.S. states. In size, Delaware is
   A. 50th
   B. 49th
   C. 46th

5. This state got its name from
   A. the Native Americans
   B. a man
   C. a company

STOP. Do NOT turn the page.

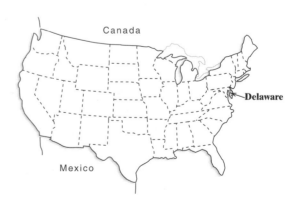

22

Exercise 15. Timed Word Selection

Directions: Read the word to the left of the line. Then read the five words to the right. Circle the word that is exactly the same as the word to the left of the line.

1.	later	late	(later)	latest	letter	lettuce
2.	island	(island)	answer	information	isn't	aisle
3.	nearby	nothing	nearer	nearest	newest	(nearby)
4.	looks	lost	look	books	desks	(looks)
5.	nine	mine	(nine)	same	name	mean
6.	long	lose	lone	alone	(long)	longer
7.	named	names	(named)	name	meaning	mended
8.	millions	million	miller	millers	(millions)	hundreds
9.	money	months	monkey	(money)	monkeys	month
10.	tons	stone	stones	tones	(tons)	sons
11.	squares	stairs	squeals	(squares)	square	statues
12.	their	there	these	they're	(their)	these
13.	died	dead	head	deaf	deal	(died)
14.	were	(were)	we're	went	west	weary
15.	this	that	these	his	(this)	things
16.	worked	working	works	(worked)	worker	wasted
17.	man	men	(man)	many	name	mean
18.	world	would	worlds	worry	(world)	worried
19.	such	sick	much	sack	touch	(such)
20.	time	times	(time)	dime	dimes	lime
21.	year	rear	young	(year)	years	younger
22.	students	studies	(students)	student	studied	student
23.	visitor	visited	visiting	visitor	vastly	monitor
24.	tuna	unit	tuna	nuts	tuba	nuts
25.	tip	top	tab	tip	type	dip

STOP. Do NOT turn the page.

Exercise 16. Timed Reading

1   The *Titanic* was a very large ship made in Britain. In fact, it was 882 feet long.
2   The *Titanic* was such a big, strong ship that most people thought that nothing could ever
3   happen to it. Unfortunately, this idea was not correct.

4   The *Titanic* is not famous because of its size. It is famous for a very sad reason.
5   On the night of April 14, 1912, the *Titanic* sank in the icy water of the North Atlantic
6   Ocean on its first trip. It was going from Britain to New York City. About 1,600 miles northeast
7   of New York City, the ship hit a large iceberg. This made a hole in the side of the ship that was
8   300 feet long. Water entered the ship through the hole, and the ship began to sink.

9   The ship sank slowly, so there was time for everyone to leave the ship. However,
10   there were not enough lifeboats for the 2,200 people. Men gave their places to women and
11   children, so most of the people who survived were women and children.   The precise
12   number of people who died in this accident is not known, but approximately 1,500 people
13   lost their lives that night.

1. The main idea of paragraph 2 (lines 4–8) is
    A. the ship sank
    B. the ship was traveling from New York to Britain
    C. the ship is well known today because it was so big

2. The word *sink* in line 8 means
    A. go down
    B. move quickly
    C. make noise

3. The reading does not say it, but we can guess that the news about the *Titanic* was a big surprise
    A. because more men than women died
    B. because people thought that this ship could not sink
    C. because everyone knew that this was a very big ship

4. The number of passengers on the *Titanic* was about
    A. 1,500
    B. 1,600
    C. 2,200

5. The number of times that the *Titanic* sailed from Britain and arrived at New York City is
    A. 0
    B. 2
    C. not known

STOP. Do NOT turn the page.

Exercise 17. Timed Word Selection

Directions: Read the word to the left of the line. Then read the five words to the right. Circle the word that is exactly the same as the word to the left of the line.

1. sink	sank	think	sang	sing	sink
2. three	tree	three	trees	trays	threes
3. soup	soup	soap	sour	sound	seed
4. heart	heard	heart	head	heat	hear
5. capital	captain	capital	carpets	capitals	captains
6. main	mean	mine	main	mind	mean
7. cover	could	cover	over	covered	couldn't
8. came	came	cane	come	camel	name
9. group	groups	green	grab	group	greatly
10. miles	meals	mills	miles	mile	smiles
11. went	went	were	want	we're	weren't
12. part	port	parts	ports	part	pardon
13. sign	sign	signs	sigh	sighs	sight
14. deals	leads	deal	lead	deals	able
15. chips	chip	chop	cheap	chips	chops
16. barber	baker	barter	barber	bakery	beeper
17. there	there	these	things	those	their
18. offices	offers	offer	office	after	offices
19. women	woman	women	warmer	worms	wisdom
20. salad	salty	saddle	sealed	sale	salad
21. inside	internal	outside	inside	insight	island
22. world's	wouldn't	worlds	wheels	world's	shouldn't
23. Canadian	Canada	Colombian	Canadian	Colombia	Cairo
24. France	French	Fran's	Francis	France	Frankfurt
25. concrete	concrete	conceal	conceit	covered	construction

STOP. Do NOT turn the page.

Exercise 18. Timed Reading

1   South Dakota is in the northern United States. It is surrounded by North Dakota,
2 Minnesota, Iowa, Nebraska, Wyoming, and Montana. The largest city is Sioux Falls, but
3 Pierre is the capital.

4   South Dakota ranks sixteenth in size. Although South Dakota is a rather large state,
5 it has very few people. The population is only about 700,000. In addition, there are only
6 about nine people per square mile. (The U.S. average is sixty-nine per square mile.)
7 Farms and ranches cover ninety percent of South Dakota.

8   Thousands visit South Dakota every year to see Mount Rushmore National
9 Memorial in the Black Hills in the southwestern part of the state. This memorial has large
10 stone faces of George Washington, Thomas Jefferson, Theodore Roosevelt, and Abraham
11 Lincoln. These faces are huge. In fact, they are sixty feet high.

12   An important year in the history of South Dakota was 1874, when gold was
13 discovered in South Dakota. Many people came to look for gold. In 1876, the Homestake
14 Gold Mine was opened. This is the oldest continuous gold mine in the world. It has
15 produced millions of tons of gold.

1. The main idea of paragraph 4 (lines 12–15) is
   A. many people came to this state to look for gold
   B. the history of this state is very difficult to understand
   C. the Homestake Gold Mine is still open now

2. The word *huge* in line 11 means
   A. very beautiful
   B. very large
   C. very old

3. The reading does not say it, but we can guess that not many tourists came to this state until
   A. Mount Rushmore was finished
   B. gold was found
   C. Pierre became the capital city

4. Fifteen other states
   A. are larger than South Dakota
   B. have more people than South Dakota
   C. found gold before South Dakota did

5. In this state, we can find a large number of
   A. gold mines
   B. farms
   C. people

STOP. Do NOT turn the page.

Exercise 19. Timed Word Selection

Directions: Read the word to the left of the line. Then read the five words to the right. Circle the word that is exactly the same as the word to the left of the line.

1. gold	good	cold	load	goat	(gold)
2. farms	fast	frame	farm	frames	(farms)
3. people	person	(people)	purple	present	papers
4. mine	mind	many	(mine)	main	mean
5. fish	flash	fresh	(fish)	fence	finch
6. times	time	(times)	dime	dimes	timed
7. every	ever	never	everyone	everything	(every)
8. daily	deals	dusty	deadly	(daily)	death
9. first	fresh	fist	thirst	worst	(first)
10. Boston	Baldwin	Britain	(Boston)	Bartholdi	Black
11. companies	continuous	construction	colonies	(companies)	chemicals
12. health	(health)	heart	steal	wealth	teeth
13. came	(came)	come	name	same	cane
14. could	called	coats	would	should	(could)
15. big	box	beg	(big)	bag	bit
16. base	face	hose	(base)	based	bases
17. about	above	(about)	aboard	abduct	abundant
18. faces	face	faced	(faces)	favorite	faucet
19. rude	door	ready	running	(rude)	crude
20. soup	soap	stoop	stop	(soup)	sour
21. high	huge	height	sigh	(high)	laugh
22. inside	outside	insider	outsider	inside	inward
23. family	famous	family	families	framed	fancy
24. as	is	us	it	at	as
25. from	from	form	forms	harm	farm

STOP. Do NOT turn the page.

Exercise 20. Timed Reading

1   Alexander Graham Bell was a famous inventor. He invented many things that we
2 use in our lives every day.

3   Bell was born in Edinburgh, Scotland, in 1847. In 1870, he and his family went to
4 Canada. In 1872, he started a school for training teachers of the deaf in Boston in the
5 United States. The next year he became a professor at Boston University. In 1877, Bell
6 married Mabel Hubbard, who had been one of his deaf students.

7   Bell invented many things, but his most famous invention is the telephone. In
8 1883, Bell invented a Graphophone (a type of record player) that played wax records. Bell
9 also worked with Glenn Curtiss, an American inventor, to develop an airplane and with
10 Casey Baldwin, a Canadian inventor, to develop a hydrofoil. (A hydrofoil is a kind of fast
11 boat.) Their hydrofoil was so successful that it set a world record for water speed in 1918.

12   Bell died in 1922. His name lives on today in the form of telephone companies
13 such as Bell South, Pacific Bell, and Bell Canada.

1. The main idea of paragraph 3 (lines 7–11) is
    A. Bell's most famous invention is the telephone
    B. the hydrofoil that Bell and Baldwin invented in 1918 was very fast
    C. Bell invented many different things by himself and with other people

2. The word _develop_ in line 9 and in line 10 means
    A. fly or drive
    B. make or produce
    C. famous or successful

3. The reading does not say it, but we can guess that
    A. both Bell and his wife were deaf
    B. Bell went to school in Scotland
    C. people are studying at Bell's training school in Boston today

4. When he died, Bell was
    A. in Canada
    B. about 75 years old
    C. not working

5. Bell Canada is the name of
    A. a school for the deaf
    B. the airplane that Bell and Curtiss invented
    C. a telephone company

STOP. Do NOT turn the page.

Exercise 21. Timed Word Selection

Directions: Read the word to the left of the line. Then read the five words to the right. Circle the word that is exactly the same as the word to the left of the line.

22

1.	cheese	chair	(cheese)	child	cream	cheap
2.	tips	pits	(tips)	tip	pit	tops
3.	tuna	nuts	ton	stone	tune	(tuna)
4.	base	case	nose	bays	boss	(base)
5.	born	(born)	brain	torn	four	form
6.	wood	weed	good	hood	(wood)	would
7.	cut	cat	cot	(cut)	gut	eat
8.	axe	oxen	box	tax	(axe)	ice
9.	silver	servant	(silver)	seven	served	slipper
10.	pointed	(painted)	points	paints	pointed	printed
11.	gold	cold	sold	bold	mold	(gold)
12.	loudly	(loudly)	cloudy	proudly	boldly	carefully
13.	chop	shop	chap	cheap	chip	(chop)
14.	afraid	after	affirm	arid	(afraid)	fried
15.	wind	(wind)	wand	went	winter	windy
16.	hands	hand	stands	lands	(hands)	land
17.	cried	tried	(cried)	fried	tries	cries
18.	trees	three	thirst	tears	(trees)	tree
19.	down	town	(down)	gown	dawn	damp
20.	began	(began)	begin	begun	bring	shrank
21.	ghost	gross	green	guest	ghosts	(ghost)
22.	about	above	aboard	(about)	abroad	April
23.	chose	chose	shoes	choose	chosen	chore
24.	poor	pear	pair	door	boot	poor
25.	forest	friends	forest	forests	friend	fortieth

STOP. Do NOT turn the page.

STRATEGY 12: Illustrations

Look at illustrations. If the reading has an illustration or picture, look at this carefully. This can give you some clues to the topic of the reading. Also, if there is any writing under the illustrations, read them carefully. Sometimes this information can help you to understand the reading better.

Exercise 22. Timed Reading

1   The Statue of Liberty is a symbol of the United States. It is recognized by people
2   from all over the world. In 1884, the people of France gave the Statue of Liberty to the
3   United States as a sign of friendship. Approximately 2 million tourists visit this famous
4   site every year.

5   The base for the statue is enormous. It is 154 feet tall. When it was finished in
6   1886, it was the largest single concrete structure in the world. It is so large inside that there
7   are stairs and an elevator. People in the United States donated money for the construction
8   of the base. It was designed by Richard Morris Hunt, a famous U.S. architect.

9   The statue is also enormous. It is 151 feet tall. It weighs over 200 tons. (One ton
10   is 2,000 pounds.) The statue was designed by Frederic Auguste Bartholdi, a French
11   sculptor, who also chose the site where the statue is still located. The internal support
12   system was designed by Alexandre Gustave Eiffel, the same man who later built the Eiffel
13   Tower in Paris.

1. The main idea of paragraph 1 (lines 1–4) is
    A. the Statue of Liberty is an important structure
    B. the people of France donated the Statue of Liberty in 1884
    C. the number of tourists who visit this structure every year is growing

2. The word *site* in line 4 and in line 11 means
    A. place
    B. statue
    C. time

3. The reading does not say it, but we can guess that
    A. the Statue of Liberty is older than the Eiffel Tower
    B. the Eiffel Tower is heavier than the Statue of Liberty
    C. both A and B   *Altura*

4. The person who selected the place where the Statue of Liberty is located also
    A. built the internal support system
    B. donated money for the construction
    C. designed the Statue of Liberty

5. Of these people, the person who was not French is
    A. Richard Morris Hunt
    B. Frederic Auguste Bartholdi
    C. Alexandre Gustave Eiffel

STOP. Do NOT turn the page.

Exercise 23. Vocabulary Recall

Read the vocabulary word in boldface print on the left. Read the three choices and choose the one that is similar in meaning or has something in common with the first word. Write the letter of the answer on the line.

	Word	A	B	C
A	1. **divide**	cut	add	make
A	2. **population**	people	money	education
B	3. **spinach**	jewelry	vegetable	education
A	4. **come up with**	answer	dictionary	classroom
B	5. **ghost**	direction	afraid	interesting
C	6. **silver**	food	smell	color
C	7. **cut down on**	nice things	light things	bad things
B	8. **slight**	price	difference	score
C	9. **island**	history	math	geography
A	10. **precise**	exact	maybe	something
B	11. **rude**	not hungry	not polite	not successful
A	12. **exercising**	sports	television	magazines
A	13. **a mine**	gold	kilometers	vegetables
B	14. **amazing**	not good	surprising	very cold
C	15. **sink**	car	airplane	ship
A	16. **prompt**	on time	very polite	well-dressed
B	17. **bay**	land	water	air
B	18. **mushrooms**	a house	food	coins
A	19. **boil**	tea	ice cream	statue
C	20. **applause**	classroom	restaurant	concert
A	21. **passengers**	airplane	hospital	sports team
A	22. **huge**	size	cost	color
C	23. **develop**	famous	drive	make
B	24. **site**	chairs	location	situation
A	25. **donate**	give	design	enormous

Explanation for Exercise 1, p. 65

1. vegetables (Carrots, broccoli, and spinach are vegetables.)
2. white, green, black, brown, silver (Many answers are possible. The answer should be a color. It should not be a crazy color. For example, pink and purple are not usual answers.)
3. giraffes, elephants, rhinos (Any popular zoo animal is OK here.)
4. fish (This is the best answer because most people keep fish in an aquarium.)
5. pie, ice cream, pudding (Any kind of dessert is OK here.)
6. Atlantic (You must use the name of a body of water. Some bodies of water are not OK. For example, there are no whales in the Caribbean Sea or in the Mississippi River.)
7. April (This is the month between March and May. This is the most logical answer.)
8. history, French (You can use the name of any school subject EXCEPT math, science, English, or geography.)
9. three (This is the most logical answer.)
10. square (You should say a shape that we use a ruler to draw. It should have lines. A circle and an oval are not good here. You need a shape with lines.)
11. strawberry, cherry (There are many possible answers. All ice cream flavors are OK EXCEPT chocolate and vanilla.)
12. water (The key word here is only. This tells us that we are talking about only the basic things you need to cook beans. Besides beans and salt, water is important.)

STRATEGY 13: Reading Speed

Why are you reading the exercise? Read fast or slowly according to your answer. If you have to answer many questions about details, then read slowly and carefully. If you are reading to find out the author's main idea or what the general topic is, then it is OK to read quickly. Read with the correct speed.

Lesson 6
Extended Reading Fluency Practices

Exercise 1. Nonprose Menu

Here is a menu from a small restaurant. Read the menu and then do part 1.

JACK'S SANDWICH SHOP

ABSOLUTELY THE BEST SANDWICHES IN TOWN

Sandwiches:*

Hamburger	$ 1.95	Chicken	2.35
Roast Beef	2.50	Egg Salad	1.50
Tuna Salad	1.60	Turkey	2.15

Drinks:

Cola	.95	Diet Cola	.95
Iced Tea	.75	Orange Juice	1.15
Milk	.95	Coffee	.50

Extras:

Side Salad	.85	Cole Slaw	.85
French Fries	.75	Potato Chips	.75
Bowl of Soup	1.55	Cup of Soup	.90

Desserts:

Cheesecake	1.75			
Apple Pie	1.50			
Ice Cream	dish 1.75		cone	.85

Sandwich Set:* Choose any sandwich, iced tea, French fries, and apple pie for only $ 4.25.

*Cheese is an extra 50¢.

Call ahead for take-out orders (11 A.M.–8:30 P.M.) 388-2219

Part 1.   Read the questions below. Find the answers in the menu and then write you[r]

1. How much does a turkey sandwich, a side salad, and a cola cost? $ 3.9?

2. In which section can you find French fries?   extras

3. If Mr. Lim is trying to lose weight, what can he drink?   Diet cola

4. If Mrs. Rivera wants to eat fish, what can she order?   tuna salad

5. How much is a roast beef sandwich, iced tea, and French fries? $4.00

6. How much is the order in number 5 if you also order apple pie? $5.50

7. What time does the restaurant open?   at 11.a.m

8. Why does this menu not have spaghetti or pizza?   Because It's a
sandwich shop

9. What is the most expensive dessert? Ice cream   How much is it? con .85

10. How much does a cheeseburger cost? $ 2.45

Part 2.   Read these ten statements about the menu on page 90. Write T on the line if the statement is true and F if the statement is false. Write DK if we don't know the answer from the information in the menu.

___T___ 1.   Cheesecake is more expensive than an egg salad sandwich.
___T___ 2.   Coffee costs half a dollar.
___DK__ 3.   Jack's Sandwich Shop sells chocolate ice cream.
___T___ 4.   A side salad is less than a dollar.
___F___ 5.   There is no extra charge for cheese on a sandwich.
___F___ 6.   The telephone number for this restaurant is at the top of the menu.
___T___ 7.   Soup and ice cream come in two different sizes.
___DK__ 8.   The soup is probably tomato soup or mushroom soup.
___F___ 9.   People who do not eat meat cannot eat any of the sandwiches in this restaurant.
___T___ 10. There is no pork on this menu.

Exercise 2. Nonfiction: Is Eating Fish Really Healthy?

Part 1.   Prereading. Answer these questions about your diet. (Diet means what you eat every day.) When you have finished, compare your answers with other students.

1. How many times in a week do you eat red meat?   1o 2

2. Is your answer to number 1 good for your health?   yes

3. Have you ever eaten fish for breakfast? _____*No*_____ If no, why not? _____*Because   sometimes*___ *only   eat   in   lunch   or   dinner* _____

4. How often do you eat dark green vegetables? ___*1 or 3   times.*___

5. Is your answer to number 3 good for your health? ___*yes*___

6. How often do you eat fish? ___*1 times   month,*___

7. Is your answer to number 6 good for your health? ___*yes*___

8. Is eating fish good for our health? Give reasons for your answer. ___*Because   is   rich*___ *in   Iron,   not   give   problems   with   colesterol* _____

Part 2.   Reading. Read this information about eating fish. Answer the questions in the boxes.

Is Eating Fish Really Good for Our Health?

For many years, doctors told us that eating fish is very good for our health. Doctors said that eating fish is good because it helps to stop heart disease. Many Americans are worried about heart disease because the United States has many cases of heart disease. (Heart disease is the number one killer in the United States.) However, a recent study does not agree with this advice about eating fish to stop heart disease.

Questions: 1. What is your reaction to this information?
 a. You are surprised.
 b. You do not like the topic.
 c. You do not understand the words.
 d. You are not surprised.

2. Look at the first sentence and the last sentence. Do these two sentences have the same information or different information?
 different

The recent study is part of three large studies at the Harvard School of Public Health. This study compared two groups. In one group are men who eat fish several times a week. In the other group are men who eat fish only once a month. This study found that men in the first group have as much heart disease as men in the second group.

Questions: 3. Who are the two groups? *I men eat fish several times a week*
- I men eat fish only once a month.

4. Which group has more heart disease?
Same

The news from this study is very surprising. In previous studies, doctors said that fish eaters live longer than people who do not eat much fish. In addition, heart disease is less common in Japan and Greenland, perhaps because fish is a big part of daily food there.

Questions: 5. Do people in the United States eat more fish than people in Greenland? Why do you say this answer? *No - Because is only part of daily food +*

6. The writer says the news from this study is surprising. Why is this news surprising? *Because fish eaters live longer than people who do not eat much fish.*

Dr. Alberto Ascherio, the main author of the report, said that eating fish is not bad for us. "But some people may be eating fish instead of eating vegetables or exercising." This is not good. Eating fish is good, but it is not enough to cut down on the number of cases of heart disease. We need to eat vegetables, too. We also need to remember to exercise.

Question 7. What does *This* in the second line of the preceding paragraph mean? *fish, eating fish*

Some people eat a lot of fish. They do this because they think that eating a little fish is good, so then eating a lot of fish is very good for us. Dr. Martijn Katan, a doctor in the Netherlands, said that perhaps this is not 100% true. A little fish may be good for us, but the doctor said that this does not mean that a lot of fish is very good for us.

"People eat a lot of fish because they think eating a little fish is good, so then eating a lot of fish is very good for us."

Question 8. Does Dr. Katan agree with this sentence? Why do you say this answer? *No Because he said that 100%*

'ine of the reading. Fill in the missing words to complete the outline for the reading. Use the
's below.

important   Dr. Katan's   a lot of   surprising
advice   Japan   several   information
longer   vegetables   place   same

I. Eating fish and heart disease
    A. Old information: eating fish helped stop heart disease

    B. New _information_: does not agree with the old information

II. Recent study

    A. _Place_: Harvard School of Public Health
    B. Method: two groups
       1. Group 1: men who ate fish _several_ times a week
       2. Group 2: men who ate fish only once a month

    C. Results: _same_ amount of heart disease in the two groups

III. Reasons the results are _surprising_

    A. Previous studies: fish eaters live _longer_

    B. _Japan_ and Greenland: people eat a lot of fish and have less heart disease

IV. Dr. Ascherio's _advice_
    A. Eating fish is good, but

    B. Eating _vegetables_ and exercise are _important_, too

V. _Dr Katan's_ advice
    A. Eating fish is good, but

    B. Eating _a lot of_ fish is not a lot better

STRATEGY 14: Italics

Look at words in italics carefully. Sometimes you
can find words in *italics* (italics). Sometimes the
name of a book is written in italics. For example,
Gone with the Wind is a famous book about the
American South. Sometimes we use italics for
emphasis. For example, when you write your
answers on this page, do not use a *pencil*. Use a
blue or black pen.

Exercise 3. Fiction

Part 1.   A folktale is a story that people in an area have told and told and told over many years. This folktale is from Thailand, but it is also told in Korea and in Japan. It is about a poor woodcutter and a special problem that he has. Read the folktale and answer the questions in the boxes.

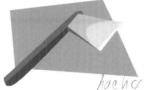

hache

The Woodcutter and His Axe (1,024 words)

Once upon a time there was a poor woodcutter. He didn't have much money, but he was a very happy man. He didn't have a big house, and he didn't have many possessions. However, he did have one possession that was very important to him. This was his <u>axe</u>. It was an old axe, and the man had used it for many years. However, the woodcutter's axe was a very good axe.

Questions: 1. Do you know this story already?
About a poor woodcutter and his axe

2. Why do you think the axe was so important to him?
Because he did have one possession)

The man did not have much education or special training, but he was very hardworking. The only thing that he knew how to do was to cut wood. His axe was very important to him. Axes were very expensive, and he had had his axe for a long time. Without his axe, he couldn't do any work at all.

One day the woodcutter went to the forest to cut down wood as he did every day. He was walking in the forest, looking for a good tree to cut down. Finally, he chose a tree that was near the river. He began to cut down the tree.

Question 3.   The river is an important part of this story. What do you think is going to happen with the river? Why do you think the river is important in this story? What is your prediction?

The poor woodcutter was cutting and cutting and chopping and chopping. He began to sweat. His hands became wet and slippery. Suddenly the axe flew out of his hands and landed in the river. The man tried to find his axe in the river. He looked and looked, but the water was moving so swiftly. He couldn't see his axe anywhere.

Questions: 4. Was your prediction correct?

5. Why was this such a bad thing for the man?

This was really a very bad situation for the poor woodcutter. He began to cry very loudly. "What am I going to do now?" asked the man. "How can I get food for my family if I can't cut down trees?" he cried out loud. He knew that without an axe, he didn't have any future.

Suddenly he heard a noise that sounded like the wind. He looked up and there was a ghost next to the tree. The ghost did not look frightening, so the man was not afraid of the ghost.

Questions: 6.   Is the man alone now? Explain your answer.

7.   What do you think is going to happen?

The ghost was holding a golden axe in his hand. The ghost pointed to the golden axe and said to the man, "Is this your axe?"

"No, that's not my axe," the woodcutter said.

The ghost held up a second axe. This one was the same size as the first one, but this one was a silver axe. The ghost pointed to the silver axe and said to the man, "Is this your axe?"

Again, the woodcutter replied, "No, that's not my axe."

Then the ghost held up a third axe. This axe was wet, and water was dripping from it. The ghost pointed to this axe and asked the man again, "Is this your axe?"

When the woodcutter saw this axe, he recognized it at once. He began to smile again. The woodcutter replied, "Yes, that is my axe."

The ghost gave the man the wet axe. The ghost also gave the man the silver axe and the golden axe.

Question 8.   Can you tell what happened in your own words?

Of course the woodcutter was so happy. He had never seen gold or silver. Now he had a golden axe and a silver axe. He ran back to the village to tell everyone what had happened.

The first person that the woodcutter met back in the village was his neighbor. His neighbor was also a woodcutter. The neighbor was so surprised to hear the woodcutter's story. The neighbor couldn't believe the woodcutter's good fortune.

After the woodcutter left, the neighbor ran to his closet. He got his axe and ran down to the same tree where the woodcutter had been a few hours ago.

Question 9.   What do you think the neighbor is going to do now?

When the neighbor reached the spot where the woodcutter had been before, he threw his axe into the river as hard as he could. He immediately began crying. "Oh, no, my good axe! It's lost forever! My poor axe! Poor me!"

At first, nothing happened, so the neighbor began to cry even louder. "OH, NO, MY AXE! MY POOR AXE! POOR ME!"

Suddenly he heard a noise that sounded like the wind. He looked up and there was a ghost next to the tree. The ghost did not look frightening, and the neighbor was not afraid of the ghost. He had

selfish
jealous
greedy
learn your lesson
be honest
be happy with what you have
don't be too ambitious –
don't worry
simple person
do right/don't lie
disrespect.
believe himself
no fear

hoped that the ghost would come, so he was very happy to see the ghost. In fact, he wanted to know why the ghost had taken such a long time to appear. The man said, "I have been crying out loud here for almost ten minutes. Where have you been?"

Question 10.   What do you think will happen next?

The neighbor saw that the ghost was holding a golden axe in his hand. The ghost pointed to the golden axe and asked the neighbor, "Is this your axe?"

"Yes, that's my axe," the neighbor said.

The ghost held up a second axe. This one was the same size as the first one, but this one was a silver axe. The ghost pointed to the silver axe and said to the neighbor, "Is this your axe?"

The neighbor replied, "Yes, oh, yes. That's my axe, too."

Then the ghost held up a third axe. This axe was wet, and water was dripping from it. The ghost pointed to this axe and asked the man again, "Is this your axe?"

When the neighbor saw this axe, he recognized it at once. This really was his axe, but he did not want this poor axe now. He wanted the golden and the silver axes. The neighbor replied, "Oh, no, that is not my axe. My axe is very different from that one."

Question 11.   Why did the neighbor say that the axe was not his?

When the ghost heard this last answer, he threw all three axes into the river. The man ran to the river. He tried and tried to find the axes in the river. He didn't find the golden axe and he didn't find the silver axe. He could not find his old axe either. He never found any of the three axes.

The ghost disappeared. The neighbor cried out for the ghost, "Please come back. I need my axe to do my work." However, the ghost never came back and the man never saw any of the three axes again.

Part 2.   Sometimes a folktale has a moral. A moral means a kind of teaching. The story can teach us something important about life.

What is the moral of this story? _____

_____

_____

_____

_____

Discuss your answer in small groups.

Part 3.   Summary Practice. Read this summary of the folktale. The folktale has 1,024 words, but this summary has only 200 words. Some of the words are missing. Fill in the blanks with a correct word.

Summary of "The Woodcutter and His Axe"

"The Woodcutter and His Axe" is a folktale that is told in many countries. In this story, a poor wood-cutter lost his (1)_____*axe*_____ in the river one day. He was very upset about this. A ghost came to him and offered him a (2)_____*golden*_____ axe. However, the woodcutter was very honest and told the (3)_____*ghost*_____ that it wasn't his axe. The ghost then offered the man a silver axe, but again the man refused to (4)_____*take*_____ it. Finally, the ghost offered the man his old wet (5)_____*axe*_____, and he said it was his. The ghost then gave the woodcutter all (6)_____*three*_____ axes.

The woodcutter told his neighbor about his (7)_____*good*_____ luck. The neighbor, who was very greedy, ran to the same spot where the (8)_____*ghost*_____ had come before. He threw his axe into the river and pretended that he had lost it. The ghost came and asked him (9)_____*about*_____ the same three axes. This man said the golden axe and the silver axe were his, but he didn't (10)_____*want*_____ his old axe. The ghost knew the man was lying and (11)_____*threw*_____ all three axes into the river. The neighbor never found any of the three axes. Now he has (12)_____*nothing*_____.

STRATEGY 15:
Prereading: Prediction

Before you read, guess what the reading is about. Good readers can use many clues (titles, illustrations or pictures, sentences) to guess the general topic of a reading. This is a very important strategy. Try to guess what you are going to read. It is easy to become a better reader with this strategy.

Exercise 4. News Reports: True or False?

Read these three news stories. Two of them are false and one of them is true. Circle true or false. Then answer the question at the end of this exercise.

1. true or false?   **Cats and Dogs Don't Always Fight**

In New Orleans, Louisiana, a cat named Minnie recently gave birth to four young animals. Of course this is not unusual at all. What is unusual about this is that the father in this case is not another cat but rather a dog! Marion Pelter, Minnie's owner, said that the father of the four young animals is her other pet, a small brown dog named Brownie. Veterinarians (animal doctors) are unable to explain how or why a dog and a cat decided to do this, but the result is very clear. Minnie and Brownie have four young of their own. "The most difficult part," said Pelter in a recent interview, "is what to call these animals. They're not kittens and they're not puppies either. Are they pittens or are they kuppies?"

2. true or false?   **Alive Again: One Boy's Amazing but True Story**

Doctors in Miami, Florida, are amazed by what happened at Miami General Hospital recently. Marcus Gent, age 13, was officially "dead" for almost 7 hours, but doctors were able to bring him back to life. Marcus was swimming at the beach with some friends when he was pulled out by the sea currents. He couldn't swim very well and soon went under the water. His friends searched for him; lifeguards at the beach found his body about 20 minutes later. He was taken to Miami General Hospital where doctors tried to revive him. Doctors continued to try for such a long time because he was a young boy. They thought that because he had a strong body, he might be able to survive. They were right. This is the first time that anyone was listed as "dead" for so many hours and came back to life. Marcus is in good condition, and doctors expect him to have only slight problems from this event.

3. true or false?   **Solving a Noise Problem with Gloves**

The organizers of a pop music concert in Hong Kong recently faced a problem situation. The organizers were planning a big concert at Hong Kong Stadium. They expected that as many as 17,500 people might attend the concert. The residents living near the stadium were very angry about all the noise that might come from the concert. These residents wanted the organizers to cancel the concert. Finally, the organizers came up with a great idea that made the residents happy. On the night of the concert, the organizers gave out 17,500 pairs of gloves for the audience to wear. When the concertgoers applauded, they didn't make so much noise, and the nearby residents were no longer angry about the concert.

I think number _3_ is true because _is more problably the solution at this problem_

_____

_____

_____

_____

Exercise 5. Reading/Discussion/Writing: Tipping

Part 1.   Read this letter from a person who has a question about tipping. Then work with a classmate to discuss your answers to the questions after the letter.

Dear Advisor,

Last night my wife and I had dinner at a restaurant not far from our home. It is a medium-size restaurant that has been owned by the same family for years. It is not one of the large restaurant chains. My wife and I both enjoy going there very much because it is a small, friendly place. We like the atmosphere very much.

The problem is the service. We know that dinnertime is perhaps their busiest time of the day, but last night the service was not very good. We had to wait a long time before a waiter came to our table. He was very nice, but he didn't do a very good job. I ordered chicken with mushrooms, but he brought me chicken with cream sauce. My wife got her main course OK, but he put the wrong kind of salad dressing on her salad. We didn't say anything to the waiter. We just ate what he brought us.

The waiter did not ask us if we wanted dessert or coffee afterward. He just brought us the check, thanked us, and smiled.

I know that 15% tip is the usual amount. I wanted to leave 10%, but my wife said we should just leave 5% to show that we were not happy. In the end, I left 10% tip. Did I do the right thing?

Steve

Part 2. Write your answers to these questions. Then discuss them with a classmate.

1. Why did Steve write this letter? *Is hot happy with the service*
2. How much tip should Steve and his wife have left? *10%*
3. Is tipping a good thing? Why or why not? *Because is part. de salary for the people.*
4. How much do you usually tip in a restaurant? What about at other places? *yes 5% 10 to 15%*
5. What are the tipping customs in your country? If they are different from the custom in this letter, which do you think is better? Why? *Is better*

Part 3. Now read these responses from four different people. Which response do you think is the best? Why? Which one is the worst? Why do you think this?

Answer 1

Dear Steve,

I eat out all the time. I have seen some very good waiters and waitresses, and I have seen some really bad ones. Your waiter doesn't sound so bad. Yes, he made some mistakes, but you didn't have to wait very long for the food, did you? To me, that's very important. I hate to wait and wait for a long time for my food.

It's a hard job. Have you ever waited on tables? You have to deal with rude people who can't make a simple decision about vegetables sometimes.

Give the waiter the tip. Don't be stingy! *Japan O*

Valerie

Answer 2

Dear Steve,

How much did the last haircut you got cost you? Were you 100% happy with the haircut? If you weren't happy, did you give the barber less than 100%? I don't think so. So why do you think it's OK to give the waiter less than the standard tip?

If the waiter was nice to you and your wife and tried to serve you well, then you should leave the tip. I don't like people who are cheap and don't leave the right tip. This is bad for all of us.

The standard tip is 15%. If you like the service, leave more. If you are not happy, leave 15%. The standard is 15%.

Sheila

Answer 3

Dear Steve,

    The waiter's job is to serve you the customer. Service is his job. If his service was not good, then you have no obligation to leave any tip. The word tip stands for "to insure promptness." In other words, we leave a tip so the waiter will know that he is going to be paid for his service. If the service is not good, then the tip is not good either. This is logical to me.

    I think you were generous. I might have left only 5% if the service had been really bad. I think a tip of only 5% would tell the waiter that something was wrong.   mesero

    Please don't leave 0%. Waiters are paid only a small amount by the restaurant. They need our tips to live on.

Walter

Answer 4

Dear Steve,

    Why didn't you tell the manager? I think I would have told the manager. It's important to tell the waiter's boss so the boss can make sure everything will be OK next time. You didn't tell the manager that there were a few problems. You didn't tell the waiter that anything was wrong. Nothing will change because no one knows there was a problem. This was a mistake.

    You left the man 10%. I think that was good but not really necessary. Why did you give a tip to someone who did not give you good service?

    In my job (I'm a brickmaker), if I make a mistake, I don't get paid for my work. This is common sense to me.   comun senti do

Henry

Part 4.   For homework, write your own reply letter to Steve. Follow the four examples in part 3. Write your own opinion. Try to limit your answer to 125 words. Be sure to say EXACTLY what you think Steve should do. Be sure to give reasons why Steve should follow your suggestions.

At the next class, pass around your papers so that everyone gets to read everyone else's letters.

Lesson 7

Reading Tasks and Vocabulary Activities

Task 1. Reading: Directions and a Map

Part 1.   Use the information in these five passages to write the names of the shops in the correct place on the map.

1. Tasha Growe works at the jewelry store. She takes the bus to work every morning. The bus is very convenient for Tasha because it stops at the corner of Broad and Pine, which is where the jewelry store is located. She sometimes eats lunch at the Mexican restaurant that is just across the street from where she works.

2. Kevin Jenks works at the furniture store. This store is between the Mexican restaurant and the bakery. He doesn't like spicy food, so he rarely eats at the Mexican restaurant. He usually eats lunch at the Chinese restaurant on the corner of Snow Street and Lucas Avenue, or sometimes he brings a sandwich from home.

3. *Travel agent:*   Here is your ticket, Mr. Jones. Have a good trip!
    Mr. Jones: Thanks. Could you tell me how to get to the post office from here? I have to mail a letter.
    Travel agent: Sure. When you go outside, turn left. At the corner, turn right and walk one block. At the next street, turn right. That's Lucas Avenue. The post office is the second door on your right.
    Mr. Jones: That doesn't sound too difficult. Thanks.

4. There is a new post office in this town. It is located on Lucas Avenue. The post office has been at this location for about a year. Before that, it was located on the corner of Snow Street and Broad Avenue. That location was too small, so the post office moved to Lucas Avenue. The old post office location is now a shoe store.

5. Yesterday Mrs. Thomas went to the florist to buy some flowers for her friend's birthday. When she left the florist, she walked to the right. The next store on her right was the bakery. She felt like eating something sweet, so she went in to get a dozen chocolate doughnuts. She paid for the doughnuts and left the bakery. She decided to go into the bookstore across the street to buy a newspaper. After that, she went home.

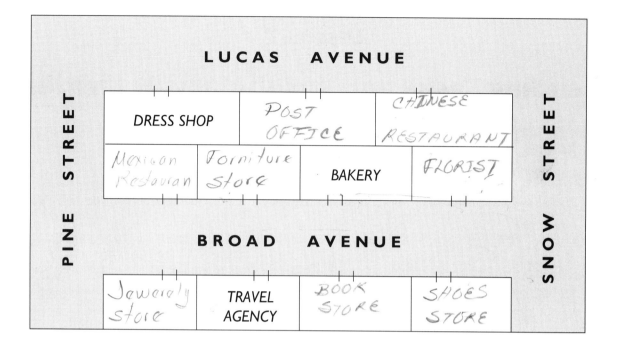

Part 2.   Read these ten statements about the map above. Write T on the line if the statement is true and F if the statement is false. Write DK if we don't know the answer from the information on the map.

_____ 1. The bakery is on Broad Avenue.

_____ 2. The travel agency is not on the same street as the dress shop.

_____ 3. The travel agency is across the street from the post office.

_____ 4. The Chinese restaurant is older than the jewelry store.

_____ 5. The shoe store is on the corner of Broad Avenue and Pine Street.

_____ 6. The dress shop is next to the post office.

_____ 7. The jewelry store is across the street from the Mexican restaurant.

_____ 8. The bookstore is next to the travel agency.

_____ 9. The post office is between the Chinese restaurant and the dress shop.

_____ 10. The furniture store is not on Lucas Avenue.

Task 2. Reading: Matching Pictures with Descriptions

An art teacher asked her twelve students to draw a picture of a street with houses and trees. In addition, the students had to write a small report about their drawings.

The drawings that the students made are on this page. However, there is a problem. The drawings do not have the students' names on them.

Read the reports and then write the students' names on their drawings. Good luck!

Name: _Belinda_ 	Name: _Stephen_ 	Name: _Susan_ 
Name: _Lee-Ann_ 	Name: _James_ 	Name: _Tanya_ 
Name: _Keith_ 	Name: _Matthew_ 	Name: _Karl_ 
Name: _David_ 	Name: _Martha_ 	Name: _Eileen_ 

Susan wrote: On my street, there are three houses. The house on the left has a white roof. The house on the right has a gray roof. There is only one tree. It is between a house with a black roof and a house with a gray roof.

Eileen wrote: My drawing is very easy to find. In my drawing, there are two houses. There are also two trees. Both of the houses have a white roof.

Matthew wrote:	In my picture, there are two houses with a white roof. There is also another house with a gray roof. The house with the gray roof is on the left. The houses with a white roof are next to each other. The tree is between the house with a gray roof and the two houses with a white roof.
Keith wrote:	On my street, there are three houses and one tree. The tree is on the left. The houses are on the right. Two of the houses have a black roof. The other house has a white roof. The two houses with a black roof are next to each other. The house with a white roof is next to the tree.
Stephen wrote:	In my drawing, there are three houses and one tree. One house has a black roof. The tree is next to this house. The other two houses have a gray roof. They are next to each other.
Lee Ann wrote:	I think it is easy for you to find my picture. My picture has two trees and two houses. One tree is on the left, and the other tree is on the right. The two houses are between the two trees. One house has a gray roof, and the other house has a white roof.
David wrote:	My picture is the only picture that has three trees. There is only one house. This house does not have a white roof and it does not have a gray roof. The roof is black.
Tanya wrote:	My picture has two houses and two trees. One tree is on the right, and the other tree is between the two houses. One house has a gray roof, and the other has a white roof. The house with a white roof is on the left. The house with a gray roof is between the two trees.
Belinda wrote:	In my drawing, there are three houses and one tree. The tree is on the right. Two of the houses have a gray roof. The other house has a white roof. The house with the white roof is between the other two houses.
Martha wrote:	On this street, there are two houses and two trees. The two trees are on the left, and the two houses are on the right. The house with a white roof is between a tree and the house with a black roof.
James wrote:	My picture has two houses and two trees. One house has a white roof. It is on the left. The other house has a gray roof. It is on the right. The two trees are next to each other. They are in the middle of the picture. They are between the two houses.
Karl wrote:	In my picture, there are three houses. Two houses have a black roof. The other house has a white roof. The house with a white roof is between the other two houses. The tree is on the right.

Task 3. Reading: Math Problems

Are you good at math? Read the following situations and then see if you can find the correct answer to the problem.

1. Mr. and Mrs. Dalton have four children. Each of their children is married, and each of their children has two children. At Christmas, the Daltons buy presents for all their children, their sons-in-law, their daughters-in-law, and their grandchildren. How many presents do they have to buy? • *16*

2. Karen took a trip to Mexico City. She stayed at the Hotel Del Angel for $40 a night. This price included breakfast, but it did not include lunch or dinner. She spent about $10 for each of these meals. The air fare from Miami to Mexico City on United Airlines was $390. She took four tours, and each tour cost her $25. She was there for a total of four full days and nights. How much money did she spend for everything? *$730*

3. Jack went to the supermarket. He bought four cans of peas, four cans of corn, and four cans of green beans. The supermarket was having a big sale, and canned vegetables were four for a dollar. He also bought a bag of potatoes for $2.50 and two heads of lettuce for eighty cents each. He wanted to buy chocolate ice cream, but it was too expensive at $4.50 a gallon, so he didn't get it. How much money did he spend? *7:10* *3.00* *3.50* *1.60*

4. Mrs. Hanks is having five people come to her house for dinner. Each person at the table will have two glasses of milk. A carton of milk has about six glasses of milk in it. How many cartons does she need to buy? *2*

5. The grading system at Bryan Elementary School is as follows: A = 95–100, B = 85 –94, C = 75–84, D = 70–74, F = below 70. Here are the scores for the last English test:

Jack Smith	88	Tasha Jones	94	Mark Wilson	73	Jenny Craven	42
Keith Benson	95	Leon Jenks	77	Shelly Warner	80	Tony Jones	100
Heather Adams	90	Sammy Price	72	Troy Smith	82	Clay Zimmer	55
Jimmy Globes	76	Betty Erwin	97	Yvonne Green	78	Emily Mount	99
Patty Young	90	Brett Erikson	61	Lance Rollins	83	Claire Wood	68

What was the most common letter grade? (A, B, C, D, or F)
How many people did not pass the test? (F = failing) *4*

6. Tommy painted the inside walls of his house three times. He wanted to sell his house, so it was important for the walls to look new, clean, and beautiful. Each time he painted the walls, he used three cans of paint. Each can of paint cost ten dollars. How much money did he spend on paint?

90

Task 4. Reading: Spelling Rules

Part 1.   Is English spelling difficult for you? Here is a small spelling quiz to see how good your spelling ability is in English.

A. Write EI or IE on the line.

1. bel*ie*ve   2. n*ei*ghbor   3. rec*ie*ve   4. ch*ie*f

5. th*ie*f   6. p*ie*rced ears   7. ach*ie*ve   8. w*ei*ght

B. Write the past tense (-ed) of these verbs.

1. stop   stopped   6. enjoy   enjoyed

2. listen   listened   7. ask   asked

3. offer   offered   8. hope   hoped

4. snow   snowed   9. prefer   prefered

5. play   played   10. try   tried

C. Write the present participle (-ing) of these verbs.

1. cut   cutting   5. meet   meeting

2. begin   beginning   6. learn   learning

3. write   writing   7. fly   flying

4. control   controling   8. erase   erasing

D. Write these words with -s.

1. I buy, he   buys   3. 1 day, 4   days   5. 1 boy, 8   boys

2. I cry, he   cries   4. 1 fly, 10   flies   6. 1 city, 2   cities

Part 2.   Now read the following passage about English spelling.

English Speling or Spelling ?

Which is correct: speling with one L or spelling with two Ls? Many students of English as a second or foreign language have problems with English spelling. (Spelling with two Ls is correct.) It is true that English spelling is difficult. However, there are rules and generalizations about English spelling. If students can learn these rules, this will help to make English spelling easier.

One of the most common spelling mistakes is with EI or IE. For example, is the correct spelling believe or beleive? Is the correct spelling receive or recieve? Is it weigh or wiegh? Many people make a mistake with this spelling, but the rule is very, very easy. The rule is I before E except after C or when sounded as the letter A as in the word weigh. Thus, the correct spelling is believe; we should put I before E. The correct spelling for the second example is receive; we should put E before I because this spelling comes after the letter C. The correct spelling for the third example is weigh because the pronunciation of these letters is like the letter A.

Another common spelling difficulty is with double letters when adding -ing or -ed. Is the correct spelling making or makking? For example, is the correct spelling cuting or cutting? Is it asked or askked? Is it begining or beginning? Is it opened or openned? The rule for doubling letters is not difficult. If the word finishes in a vowel (a, e, i, o, u, y) or w, do not double the letter. (If a word finishes in E, drop the E, but do not double the letter.) Thus, the correct spelling is making; drop the e but do not double the k. If the word finishes in one consonant (b, c, d, f, etc.), double the consonant. Therefore, the correct spellings are cutting and asked; double the consonant only if there is one consonant. The last examples are a little difficult because the words have two syllables. Say "begin." The stress (loud sound) is on the second syllable: be GIN. If the stress is on the second syllable, then double the final consonant. Say "open." The stress is on the first syllable: O pen. If the stress is on the first syllable, do not double the final consonant.

A third common spelling problem for English learners is what to do with a word that ends in Y when we add -s or -ed. Is the correct spelling storys or stories? Is the correct spelling played or plaied? The rule for this problem is very easy. If the letter before the Y is a consonant, then change the Y to I and add ES or ED. Thus, the correct spelling is stories because R is a consonant. If the letter before the Y is a vowel, then do not change the Y; just add -s or -ed. Thus, the correct spelling is played because A is a vowel.

Part 3.   Now use the information in this reading to check your answers for part 1.

Part 4.   Discussion. In small groups, discuss your answers and thoughts about the questions below.

1. Which of the three spelling rules in the reading is the most difficult for you? Can you think of more examples of the rule?

2. Which of the three rules is the most useful in your writing? Why?

3. What is the hardest word for you to remember how to spell correctly in English? _____

    Take turns saying your word for your classmates to see how many of them are able to spell your word. Whose word is the most difficult for the class to spell?

4. How does English spelling compare with spelling in your own language? Are there words that are commonly misspelled? Why are they misspelled?

5. Is there another spelling rule that you would like to know? Ask your teacher or classmates if anyone knows of other rules to help all of us with English spelling.

STRATEGY 16: Vocabulary: Review

Review vocabulary all the time. It is extremely important to review the words you have learned. It is important to do this every day. It is much better to review 20 words every day than to suddenly review 140 words once a week. (Reminder: Are you keeping a vocabulary notebook? See strategy 9 on page 71.)

STRATEGY 17: Word Parts

Use word parts to help you with unknown words. What does *triplets* mean in this sentence: *The triplets keep Mrs. Beams busy.* Well, one way to start the guessing process, is to cut the word into parts. The most important part is *tri*. What does *tri* mean?   It means *three* (other examples: tricycle, triangle).   Triplets means three babies born at the same time. Sometimes the word parts inside a word can help readers understand important vocabulary. What are other word parts that you know? Make a list.

Task 5. Crossword Puzzle 1

Use the clues below the puzzle to fill in the squares with the correct letters.

Clues

Across

1. the opposite of safe
6. the opposite of down
8. at the end of a letter sometimes
9. you hear with this
12. Let's _____ the afternoon at the beach.
13. a _____ of the world
16. A flamingo _____ only one egg. (page 14)
17. A purple car is very _____.

Down

2. I _____ a student
3. the opposite of stop
4. Rare is the _____ of common.
5. Students _____ pens and paper in class.
6. abbreviation for United Airlines
7. the correct thing to do (page 48)
9. past tense
10. the number of people in a place

Across (cont.)

18. If you don't know a word, you can look it _up_ in the dictionary.

19. _Ice_ cream

21. It's time to _eat_ lunch.

24. Beethoven's country of origin (page 7)

26. Ohyo found a bird in a _____. (page 26)

28. abbreviation for the state of Georgia

29. _It_ home

31. _On_ Monday

33. _An_ egg or _an_ umbrella

34. can't hear

35. Please do this _non_

36. Austen's occupation (page 48)

Down (cont.)

11. afternoon or evening

14. abbreviation for the state of Alabama _AL_

15. the opposite of bright for colors

17. _re_ write = to write again

20. The _flag_ of Mexico is red, white, and green.

22. how old you are _age_

23. Faulkner said he was just a _farmer_. (page 16)

25. similar to a mouse

27. How much money did you _pay_ for this?

29. an insect

30. Please turn _off_ the TV when the show is over.

32. Can people swim when they are asleep?

33. chemical symbol for gold

34. Did you _do_ your homework?

Task 6. Vocabulary Building

Read the sentence and write the word on the line at the left. Change one letter of your word to make the answer for the next sentence. The first examples have been done for you. Good luck!

1. _read_ _lead_   Every morning I _read_ the morning newspaper.

    dead _moris_   The opposite of alive is _dead_.

    dear   The word that begins almost all letters is _dear_.

    deer   A _deer_ is a kind of animal.

    deep   He can't swim very well, so he doesn't go in water that is very _deep_.

2. _wood_   We use _wood_ to make houses.

good   I liked the movie. I thought it was very _good_.

gold   A long time ago, people used _gold_ instead of money.

golf   _golf_ is a game that began in Scotland.

wolf   In the children's story, the _wolf_ ate Little Red Riding Hood's grandmother.

3. _cat_   My first pet was a _cat_.

cut   When I was shaving this morning, I _cut_ myself.

cup   Would you like a _cup_ of coffee?

pup   A baby dog is called a puppy or a _pup_.

pop   Let's _pop_ some popcorn! I'm hungry!

4. _card_   Do you have a credit _card_?

care   Take _care_. See you later!

fare   How much is the bus _fare_ from here to downtown?

fame   _fame_ is the noun for the word famous.

game   We went to the basketball _game_ last night. It was great!

STRATEGY 18: Frequent Words

If a word that you don't know appears many times in a reading, try to guess its meaning. If you are not sure that you are correct, then look the word up in your dictionary. A word that is used frequently is very important to know.

Task 7. Vocabulary Building

Read the sentence and write the word on the line at the left. Change one letter of your word to make the answer for the next sentence. Good luck!

1. _fall_   In _fall_, the leaves turn red and yellow.

   ball   A Ping-Pong _ball_ is white and is made of plastic.

   bell   When the _bell_ rings, we have to go into class.

   belt   He's wearing black shoes and a black _belt_.

   melt   The weather is warmer now, so the snow is beginning to _melt_.

2. _call_   I want to make a telephone _call_.

   ball   To play baseball, you need a bat and a _ball_.

   bald   A man who doesn't have any hair is _bald_.

   bold   Dark, strong letters are called _bold_ print.

   cold   Summer is hot, but winter is _cold_.

3. _Mail_   I'm going to the post office to _send_ this letter.

   tail   That monkey has a long _tail_.

   tall   The opposite of short is _tall_.

   talk   I'd like to _talk_ to you later about a problem I have.

   walk   If the weather is good, I sometimes _walk_ to school.

4. _red_   My favorite color is _red_.

   bed   There are two pillows on my _bed_.

   bad   The opposite of good is _bad_.

   bat   A baseball _bat_ is usually made of wood.

   rat   A _rat_ is similar to a mouse.

Task 8. Vocabulary Building

Read the sentence and write the word on the line at the left. Change one letter of your word to make the answer for the next sentence. Good luck!

1. _boots_   _boots_ are smaller than ships.

    boots   Cowboys wear _boots_ .

    books   There are thousands of _books_ in a library.

    looks   Of course Joe _looks_ like Sam. They are twins.

    cooks   She usually _cooks_ scrambled eggs for breakfast.

2. _wide_   The old streets are narrow. The new streets are _wide_ .

    ride   I learned to _ride_ a bicycle when I was 6 years old.

    rice   You put gravy on potatoes or _rice_ .

    rise   Tomorrow the sun will _rise_ at 6 A.M. and set at 7:10 P.M.

    rose   A nice gift for Valentine's Day is a beautiful red _rose_ .

3. _head_   A baby doesn't usually have any hair on its _head_ .

    hear   I couldn't _hear_ the TV, so I turned it up.

    bear   A _bear_ is a big animal that lives in the forest.

    pear   A _pear_ is a yellow fruit that tastes like an apple.

    wear   What color shirt are you going to _wear_ to the party?

4. _salt_   _salt_ and pepper shakers are on every table.

    sale   The Smiths are moving, so their house is for _sale_ .

    safe   The opposite of dangerous is _safe_ .

    cafe   We ate lunch at a small _cafe_ near the university.

    cake   I love to eat chocolate _cake_ with a cup of hot coffee.

Task 9. Vocabulary Building

Read the sentence and write the word on the line at the left. Change one letter of your word to make the answer for the next sentence. Good luck!

1. _red_   The colors of the U.S. flag are _red_, white, and blue.
   bed   There are two pillows on the _bed_.
   bad   Eating too much salt is _bad_ for your health.
   sad   The opposite of happy is _sad_.
   sat   Some people _sat_ on the sofa because there were no more chairs.

2. _tape_   I used some _tape_ to close the envelope.
   take   Do you _take_ a shower at night or in the morning?
   make   Is it difficult to _make_ an omelette?
   male   The opposite of female is _male_.
   mile   Running one _mile_ every day is good exercise.

3. _ten_   We had a dozen doughnuts, but someone ate two of them, so now we only have _ten_.
   tan   _tan_ is light brown.
   man   The police are looking for a _man_ who robbed the bank this morning. He is 5'10" tall, was wearing a red and gray jacket, and has brown hair and green eyes.
   map   All geography books have a _map_ in them.
   mop   He used a _mop_ and a bucket to clean the kitchen floor.

4. _went_   Last year we _went_ to Mexico for vacation.
   west   California is located on the _west_ coast of the United States.

best   This is great! It's the _best_ apple pie I've ever tasted!

belt   You wear a _belt_ around your waist.

felt   I left work early yesterday because I _felt_ a little sick.

Task 10. Crossword Puzzle 2

Use the clues below the puzzle to fill in the squares with the correct letters.

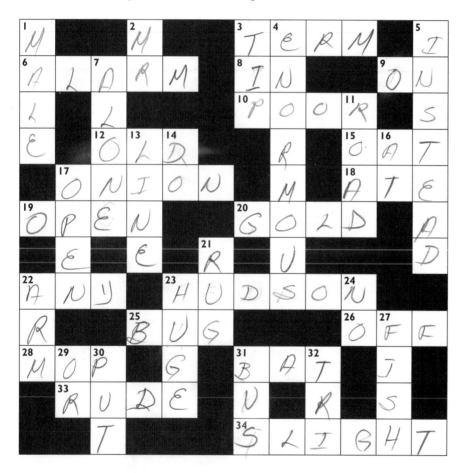

Clues

Across

3. a word or phrase _TERM_

6. an _ALARM_ clock

8. _in_ June

9. _on_ my birthday

Down

1. a boy or a man

2. _MR_, Mrs., Ms.

3. the extra money you give the waiter or waitress

4. very, very, very big

Across (cont.)

10. the opposite of rich *poor*

12. not new *old*

15. a kind of grain *oat*

17. it makes you cry when you cut it *onion*

18. We _____ lunch an hour ago.

19. the same as 17 down

20. a very valuable metal *Gold*

22. Do you have _*any*_ stamps?

23. the first European to go to Delaware (page 74) *Henry Hudson*

25. another name for insect *- Bug*

26. Can you turn _*off*_ the lights when you leave?

28. clean the floor with water *Mop*

31. something a baseball player uses *Bat*

33. not polite *RUDE*

34. a _*slight*_ difference = a small difference

Down (cont.)

5. I want tea _*INSTEAD*_ of coffee.

7. only one person

11. street *ROAD*

13. Write your name on the _*line*_ at the top of the test paper.

14. I don't like to _*do*_ the dishes.

16. _*AT*_ 7:35

17. It's hot in here. _*Open*_ the windows!

21. on the floor *RUG*

22. important body part for a baseball player *ARM*

23. very big *huge*

24. Can cats speak English? *No*

27. food discussed on page 92 *Fish*

29. Do you want coffee _*or*_ tea?

30. Please _*put*_ on your shoes.

31. some people take this every day *bus*

32. three: a _*tri*_angle

STRATEGY 19:
Ask Yourself Questions

Before you read and while you are reading, ask yourself questions. Good readers really do this all the time they are reading. Before you begin, ask yourself "What is the topic? What is this about? What does the title mean? Do I know anything about this? Have I heard this news before?" While you read, ask yourself "Is this reading about what I thought it was about? What is this reading about? Is it interesting? Is it surprising? Do I like this reading? Do I agree with the information?"

Lesson 8

Short Story: The Lady or the Tiger?

Exercise 1. Vocabulary

Here are some vocabulary words that you might need to understand this story. In each of these sentences, you will find an italicized word or group of words. Read the sentence and then write your guess about the meaning of the word. Then look up the word in a dictionary and write the real meaning.

1. He did the important job *right away*.

   YOUR GUESS: ___Now___   REAL MEANING: ___Inmediatly___

2. Your answers on the test are *perfect.* Your score is 100.

   YOUR GUESS: ___EXCELLENT___   REAL MEANING: _____

3. Please go to the bank *immediately.* You need to pay this bill now.

   YOUR GUESS: ___RIgh Now___   REAL MEANING: _____

4. This computer *system* is difficult to use.

   YOUR GUESS: ___PROGRAM___   REAL MEANING: _____

5. *Justice* for all people is important.

   YOUR GUESS: ___equality___   REAL MEANING: _____
   be fair

6. They play football in the *arena.* It can hold 3,000 people.

   YOUR GUESS: ___Stadium___   REAL MEANING: _____

7. The child was *punished* for not doing his work.

   YOUR GUESS: ___discipline___   REAL MEANING: _____
   warning
   corrected.

119

8. The child was *rewarded* for making good grades in school.

   YOUR GUESS: _Prize gratification/money_ REAL MEANING: _____

9. He met Paul at the store *by chance*. He was surprised to see Paul there.

   YOUR GUESS: _luck/ did not expect_ REAL MEANING: _____

10. The man was *accused* of killing his friend.

    YOUR GUESS: _blamed/targeted_ REAL MEANING: _____

11. These two cars are *alike*.

    YOUR GUESS: _same/similar/equal_ REAL MEANING: _____

White Bengal Tiger

12. A tiger is a *fierce* animal.

    YOUR GUESS: _wild_ REAL MEANING: _____

13. Fried chicken is *suitable* food for a picnic.

    YOUR GUESS: _appropiate right/correct_ REAL MEANING: _____

14. The police are looking for the *criminal*.

    YOUR GUESS: _law breaker Killer_ REAL MEANING: _____

15. The ending of the movie is *uncertain*.

    YOUR GUESS: _No sure No clear_ REAL MEANING: _____

16. Parents want to *protect* their children.

    YOUR GUESS: _to care/ to watch over to prevent_ REAL MEANING: _____

17. He is a very *handsome* man.

    YOUR GUESS: _attractive good looking_ REAL MEANING: _____

18. The policeman was very *brave*.

    YOUR GUESS: _strong and smart_ REAL MEANING: _____

19. What is the *relationship* of Mary Brown and Joe Brown?

    YOUR GUESS: _link/related_ REAL MEANING: _____

20. The police put the criminal in *prison*.

    YOUR GUESS: _jail_ REAL MEANING: _____

21. A diamond ring is not an *ordinary* gift.

    YOUR GUESS: _common_ REAL MEANING: _____

22. A black dress is very *elegant*.

    YOUR GUESS: _very formal/lovely_ REAL MEANING: _____

23. She *denied* taking the money.

    YOUR GUESS: _lying/refuse_ REAL MEANING: _____

24. The stores were *packed* because there was a big sale.

    YOUR GUESS: _filled/full/crowded_ REAL MEANING: _____

25. This book is expensive. *Thus*, I cannot buy it.

    YOUR GUESS: _therefore/so_ REAL MEANING: _____

26. The gift for Mr. Miles is a *secret*. Don't tell anyone.

    YOUR GUESS: _unknown/surprise_ REAL MEANING: _____

27. I am *nervous* because I have my driver's license test today.

    YOUR GUESS: _afraid/stressed_ REAL MEANING: _____

28. It rained *briefly* this morning. It only lasted 5 minutes.

    YOUR GUESS: _short duration_ REAL MEANING: _____

29. I need more gas. My gas tank is almost *empty*.

    YOUR GUESS: _nothing/finish_ REAL MEANING: _____

30. The children *screamed* when they saw the monster.

    YOUR GUESS: _yelled/shouted_ REAL MEANING: _____

31. I don't like *horror* movies.

    YOUR GUESS: _scary_ _____ REAL MEANING: _____

32. I have a *headache.* I need some aspirin.

    YOUR GUESS: _pain in your head_ REAL MEANING: _____

33. Some people believe there are angels in *heaven.*

    YOUR GUESS: _sky, God's home_ REAL MEANING: _____

Exercise 2. Story

This is a simplified version of a short story called "The Lady or the Tiger?" It was written in 1882 by Frank Stockton. When it first came out, the story was very controversial. Although Stockton wrote many things in his life, this is the story that he is best remembered for.

Now read the story. Can you answer the question that is in the title of this story?

The Lady or the Tiger? (2,262 words)

Question 1.	What do you think this story is about?

A long, long time ago, there was a special country with a king who was also very special. This king was totally in control of the country. Whatever the king wanted, he got it. If he wanted someone to do something, that person did it right away. No one asked any questions; everyone did what the king said to do. The king loved for everything to be perfect. If something was not perfect, he would change it immediately to make it correct.

One of the unique things about this country was its system of justice. The king himself had started this system. There was a large arena where people who had done bad things were punished and where people who had done good things were rewarded. This system was unique because the decision whether someone had done something good or something bad was made by chance.

When someone had done something so bad that the king was interested in the case, the person had to go to the arena. A special day was chosen and everyone in the country was told about the date and the time. The people in the country loved to go to the arena to see the justice system. The king loved to see this system because it was his own invention.

All of the people came to the arena. The king was also there, with other important members of his family and group. The king gave a signal with his hand, and a door on one side of the arena opened. The person who was accused of doing something bad came out of the door. He walked straight out of the door to the middle of the circle. On the other side of the arena in front of him, there were two doors. The two doors were near each other. They were exactly alike. They were the same color, the same shape, and the same size. The man could open either of the doors. He had to choose the door by himself. His choice was one hundred percent luck.

Question 2.	What do you think was behind the doors?

Behind one of the doors, there was a big, fierce, hungry tiger. The tiger had not been given any food for a few days, so it was very hungry. The king tried to find the biggest and strongest tiger possible. If the person opened this door, the tiger jumped out and ate him immediately. Justice was decided very quickly and by chance. If he opened this door, all of the churches in the country rang their sad bells for this poor man. All of the people in the arena went home with their heads down. Everyone was sad because someone so young or someone so old had died such a terrible way.

Question 3.	Explain what happened to the man if he chose this door.

Behind the other door, however, there was a beautiful woman. The woman was well educated and from a very good family. The king tried to find the most beautiful and most suitable woman possible. If the person opened this door, the woman came out and the man and the woman were married immediately. Young children threw flowers on the street as the new husband and wife went to their home. Justice was decided very quickly and by chance. If he opened this door, all of the churches in the country rang their loud bells for this lucky man. All of the people went home with happy thoughts in their heads and happy feelings in their hearts. Everyone was so happy that someone so young or someone so old was going to have such a good life.

Question 4.	What happened if the man chose this door?

It is clear that this system is fair. The criminal could not know where the tiger was and where the woman was. He could open either door. The choice was completely his own. In the next minute, he did not know if he would be eaten by the tiger or married to the woman. The person could not run away from this justice. Justice happened quickly. If he chose the tiger, he was killed immediately. If he chose the woman, he was married immediately.

Question 5.   Was this system of punishment fair? Why or why not?

The people in the country loved this system. It was extremely popular. When they went to the arena on justice day, they did not know if they would see a bloody death or a happy wedding.

Question 6.   Why do you think people liked this system so much?

The ending of the event was uncertain. However, the people liked the fact that the ending event was uncertain. They liked not knowing. Not knowing the ending before they went to the arena made the justice arena more interesting for them.

The king had one daughter, and it is easy to understand why she was very, very special to him. This princess was very beautiful, and she was similar to the king in many ways. Of course the king would do anything to protect his daughter. He loved her more than any other living thing on the earth.

Question 7.   What do you think is going to happen in this story next?

There was a young man who also loved the princess. He was a good man, but he was not from a rich or important family. The princess, however, did not care about these things. She was satisfied with this young man because he was handsome and he was brave. Her love for this young man was very, very strong. Both the princess and the young man were very happy with each other.

One day, unfortunately, the king learned that the princess liked this young man. When he found out, he was not happy. He did not want to lose his daughter to anyone, so he did what he had to do. He did what we expected him to do. The young man was put in prison. The king chose a day for the man to go to the justice arena. Of course everyone in the country was very interested in this case. This was not an ordinary or usual case. This case was very special because the man was in love with the king's daughter.

The king looked all over the country to find the biggest, strongest, and fiercest tiger possible. He also looked all over the country to find the most beautiful and most elegant young woman to be the man's bride.

Everyone in the country knew that the man had loved the princess. He did not deny this. The princess did not deny this. In fact, no one denied this fact. However, the king did not listen to this fact. The king wanted to use the justice arena as they had always done. The justice arena gave the king a great deal of happiness and satisfaction. For the king, the justice arena was the best system in this case. If the young man chose the tiger, the king would have his daughter. If the young man chose the woman, the king would still have his daughter. For the king, the arena was the best because he was sure that the young man would be out of the princess's life forever. More than anything, the king wanted his daughter back.

Question 8.   Explain the king's feelings about this situation.

The young man's day in the justice arena arrived. The arena was packed. People came from all over the country to see the day's event in the justice arena. There were so many people who came that they could not all fit inside, so hundreds of people were outside the arena walls waiting to know the future of this young man who had loved the princess. Of course the king was there, too. He had come to the arena with his family and important friends.

Everything was ready. The king gave the signal. The large door opened, and the princess's young man walked out from the door. He was bold, he was handsome, he was a gentleman. Half of the people had never seen such a great young man, and they understood why the princess loved him! What a terrible thing for this young man to be in the arena!

The young man walked into the middle of the arena. He turned to the king as was the custom in this country. The young man's eyes, however, did not look at the king. Instead, the young man's eyes turned to the princess, who sat to the right of her father.

Some people thought that the princess might not come to the arena this day. They thought that this was such a terrible day for her and for the young man that she might not want to see the ending of today's justice event. However, the princess was too interested not to come. From the moment that the young man was put in prison, the princess had spent every day and every night thinking about this one day.

The princess was a very, very powerful young woman. She used her power to do something that nobody had ever done before.

Question 9.	What do you think she was able to do?

The princess was able to learn what was behind each of the two doors. She knew where the tiger was and she knew where the beautiful bride was. The doors were very heavy and very thick, and no sound came out from behind them. Thus, no one could hear what was behind the doors. No one could know what was behind the doors. However, the princess, using all her power and her gold, was able to learn this secret.

The princess knew which door had the lady behind it, and she also knew who the lady was. She was one of the most beautiful and most charming ladies in the whole country, and the princess hated her. Many times the princess thought that she had seen the young woman looking at her friend, and sometimes she thought that he was also looking at the young woman. Sometimes she had seen the two talking. It was only for a moment or two, but many things can be said in a short time. Perhaps they were talking about simple, unimportant things, but how could she know? The princess had seen the young woman look at him before. With all her heart, she hated this young woman who was waiting nervously behind one of the doors.

When the young man walked to the middle of the arena, he looked up at the princess. Their eyes met for a brief moment. In this brief moment, the young man understood immediately that the princess knew which door the terrible tiger was behind and which door the lovely lady was behind. He had expected her to know because he knew the princess so well. He knew that she would not stop until she learned the secret. His only chance of life was that the princess learn the secret, and when their eyes met, he knew that she had indeed done it. He knew that she had the information that he needed now so badly.

His eyes looked at hers and asked "Which?" No word was spoken, but she heard his question very clearly. The question was asked very quickly; she must answer it as quickly.

Her right arm was resting on the side of the large chair that she was sitting in. She raised her arm and made a small, quick movement to the right. The only person who saw her arm make this movement was the brave young man. Everyone else in the arena was watching him, not her.

He then turned and walked across the empty space. He reached the two doors. He did not wait, not even a second. He was so certain of his choice. He went to the door on the right, and he opened it.

Now the point of the story is this: Did the tiger come out of the door, or did the lady?

The more we think about this question, the more difficult it is to answer. We need to think of the human heart and of human feelings and emotions. We need to think of the princess who loved this young man so much. The princess was very jealous of the other woman, but she had no hope of keeping him. She had lost him, but who should have him now?

In the last few weeks, she had often thought of the fierce tiger jumping out. She had imagined the screams, the blood, the horror. She covered her face with her hands as she thought of the person she loved so much meeting such a terrible death.

But many more times she had seen him at the other door! Her heart ached as she saw him smile when he opened the door and the tiger did not jump out. Instead, there was the lady! She saw him hold the lady. She saw him walk out to the center of the arena with her. She heard the happy shouts and cries of the thousands of people who were there that day. She heard the loud, happy bells outside the arena, and she saw him marry the lady right there.

Wouldn't it be better for him to die immediately and go to wait for her in heaven?

But she thought again about the terrible tiger, standing there with its sharp white teeth and fierce eyes. Those screams! That blood!

It is true that she pointed to the door on the right in an instant, but her decision had taken her many days and many nights of difficult thinking. She knew that he would ask her, she decided that she would answer, and without waiting even a second, she moved her hand to the right.

The question of her decision is not an easy one to think about, and it is not for me to tell you the answer directly. And so I leave the question with you: Which came out of the opened door: the lady or the tiger?

Question 10.   So what was behind the door: the lady or the tiger?

STRATEGY 20: Questions First

If you have to answer questions at the end of the reading, try reading the questions first sometimes. This is not useful for all readers, but some people like to look at the questions first. This helps the readers to focus more on the exact details and ideas of the reading passage.

Reading Rate Charts

Timed Word Selection Exercises (13, 15, 17, 19, 21)

1. Find the lesson and exercise you are doing in the top row.
2. Find your score in the left column. (Remember: Your score is the number of correct answers *minus* any mistakes.)
3. Place a dot (•) where the two lines meet.
4. After you do another exercise, connect the dots.

Examples:
Lesson 1, ex. 13: 24 correct, 1 mistake (=23)
Lesson 1, ex. 15: 25 correct, 1 mistake (=24)
Lesson 1, ex. 17: 23 correct, 2 mistakes (=21)

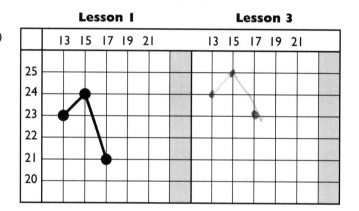

Timed Reading Exercises (14, 16, 18, 20, 22)

1. In the top row, find the lesson and exercise you are doing.
2. Write your number of correct answers under the exercise number.
3. Put an X in the squares to show which question(s) you had wrong.

Examples:
Lesson 1, ex. 14: 3 correct, #2, #4 wrong
Lesson 1, ex. 16: 4 correct, #4 wrong
Lesson 1, ex. 18: 5 correct, none wrong

	Lesson 1						**Lesson 3**				
	14	16	18	20	22		14	16	18	20	22
Correct	3	4	5								
1											
2	X										
3							X				
4	X	X						X			
5									X		

Timed Word Selection Rate Chart

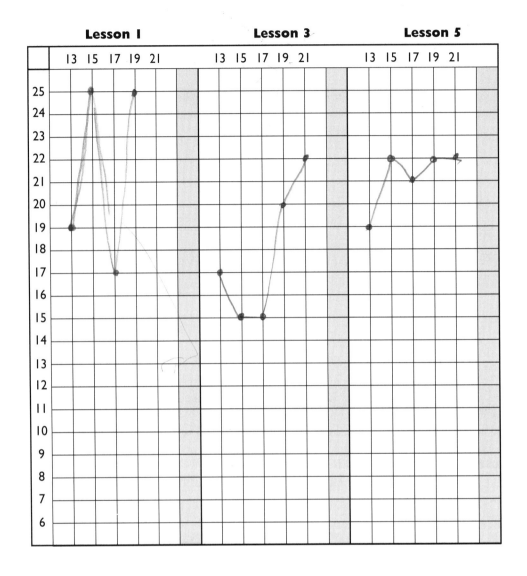

Timed Reading Rate Chart

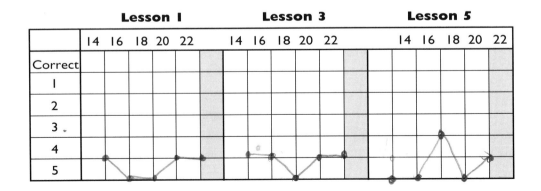

Answer Key

Lesson 1

Exercise 1, p. 1: see p. 21.

Exercise 2, p. 2: 1. C 2. A 3. A 4. B 5. C 6. C

Exercise 3, p. 2: Answers vary.

Exercise 4, p. 4: 1. and 2. but 3. and 4. so

Exercise 5, p. 5: 1. but 2. so 3. and 4. so 5. but 6. and (or so) 7. and 8. but 9. so 10. but 11. so 12. and

Exercise 6, p. 6: 1. B 2. D 3. A 4. A

Exercise 7, p. 6: 1. B 2. B 3. A 4. B

Exercise 8, p. 7: 1. C 2. A

Exercise 9, p. 8: 1. delete "The weather in this area of the United States is very dry."; A 2. delete "The trap was made of wood."; B

Exercise 10, p. 8: 1. B 2. B

Exercise 11, p. 9: 1. first A, third B, first C 2. second A, first B, second C 3. third A, second B, third C 4. fourth A, fourth B, fourth C

Exercise 12, p. 10:

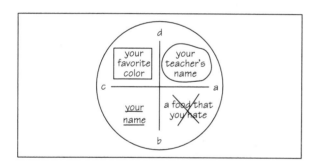

Exercise 14, p. 12: 1. C 2. A 3. A 4. A 5. C

Exercise 16, p. 14: 1. B 2. A 3. B 4. B 5. A

Exercise 18, p. 16: 1. A 2. B 3. A 4. A 5. A

Exercise 20, p. 18: 1. A 2. C 3. C 4. A 5. C

Exercise 22, p. 20: 1. A 2. B 3. A 4. A 5. B

Exercise 23, p. 21: 1. B 2. C 3. A 4. A 5. B 6. B 7. C 8. B 9. A 10. A 11. B 12. B 13. A 14. C 15. C 16. A 17. B 18. B 19. B 20. A 21. A 22. C 23. B 24. A 25. A

Lesson 2

Exercise 1, p. 22: 1. in the Language Lab 2. 12:00–12:50 3. 9 4. Intermediate Conversation 5. Beginning Conversation 6. 104 7. no 8. Jones 9. Conversation 10. A2 11–15. Questions and answers will vary.

Exercise 2, p. 24:

Part 1: 1. the United States 2. Texas 3. New York 4. 3 5. 5

Part 2: quickly, name, state, Houston, not

Part 3: I.B. 30 II.A. northeast III. Florida III.A. southeast III.B. Population IV. Texas IV.A. south central IV.B. 17 million V. Iowa V.A. Location: midwest V.B. Population: 3 million

Exercise 3, p. 26:

Part 1: Answers vary.

Part 2: Answers vary. (Possible morals: Don't be greedy. Trust people who are helping you.)

Part 3: Answers may vary. (Possible answers: 1. found 2. he 3. house 4. her 5. they 6. situation 7. market 8. cloth 9. time 10. wife 11. said 12. sad)

Exercise 4, p. 28: Number 3 is true.

Exercise 5, p. 30: Answers vary.

Lesson 3

Exercise 1, p. 33: see p. 53.

Exercise 2, p. 34: 1. B 2. A 3. B 4. B 5. A 6. A

Exercise 3, p. 34: Answers vary.

Exercise 4, p. 36: 1. It (library) 2. he (Gehrig) 3. They, they (penguins) 4. them, them (books) 5. it (war) 6. It (giraffe) 7. I (Underhill), it (theft)

Exercise 5, p. 37: 1. He 2. they 3. They, They 4. them 5. them 6. he 7. It 8. She, They (or She) 9. he, she 10. it

Exercise 6, p. 38: 1. A 2. D 3. A 4. A

Exercise 7, p. 38: 1. D 2. B 3. B 4. A

Exercise 8, p. 39: 1. D 2. A

Exercise 9, p. 40: 1. delete "An African lion is much stronger than an Indian tiger."; A 2. delete "The test has 40 questions."; C

Exercise 10, p. 40: 1. C 2. B

Exercise 11, p. 41: 1. first A, fourth B, first C 2. second A, third B, second C 3. third A, first B, fourth C 4. fourth A, second B, third C

Exercise 12, p. 42:

(triangle with X)	(circle, L?)	Your name
The month you were born	Your favorite sport to watch	Your favorite vegetable

Exercise 14, p. 44: 1. B 2. B 3. A 4. A 5. B

Exercise 16, p. 46: 1. A 2. C 3. A 4. B 5. B

Exercise 18, p. 48: 1. C 2. B 3. A 4. B 5. A

Exercise 20, p. 50: 1. A 2. A 3. A 4. A 5. C

Exercise 22, p. 52: 1. A 2. B 3. A 4. C 5. B

Exercise 23, p. 53: 1. A 2. B 3. B 4. B 5. A 6. A 7. B 8. C 9. A 10. B 11. C 12. B 13. B 14. C 15. B 16. B 17. C 18. B 19. A 20. B 21. A 22. C 23. A 24. C 25. B

Lesson 4

Exercise 1, p. 54: 1. Lincoln 2. 12 3. Garfield, Kennedy, Taylor 4. between Madison and Roosevelt; names are written in alphabetical order by last name 5. Monroe 6. Washington 7. Johnson 8. Jefferson, Madison, Monroe, Taylor, Tyler, Washington 9. various answers 10. various answers

Exercise 2, p. 55:

Part 1: 1. male 2. 17 feet or 5.2 meters 3. true 4. false 5. false 6. false 7. true 8. false 9. false 10. false

Part 3: I.B. 14 feet tall II.A. Color II.B. dust II.C. Lips II.D. bones II.E. Legs III. Baby giraffes III.A.2. Pregnant IV.B. Place V. Protection V.B. Enemies VI.A. diet

Exercise 3, p. 58:

Part 1: Answers vary; Mr. Potts. Officer Underhill did not say which painting was missing. When Mr. Potts arrived, Underhill was surprised because Potts began talking about *Roses by the Window*, but it was not possible for Potts to know this was the missing painting if he had not taken it.

Part 2: Answers vary.

Part 3: Answers may vary. (Possible answers: 1. called 2. front 3. lock 4. painting 5. were 6. museum 7. keys 8. Jackson 9. returned 10. and)

Exercise 4, p. 61: Number 2 is true.

Exercise 5, p. 62: Answers vary.

Lesson 5

Exercise 1, p. 65: see p. 89.

Exercise 2, p. 66: 1. C 2. B 3. B 4. A 5. C 6. A

Exercise 3, p. 67: Answers vary.

Exercise 4, p. 69: 1. this (South Dakota), this (Pierre) 2. These (thousands of people), this (South Dakota) 3. This (Homestake Gold Mine), this (gold) 4. this (Statue of Liberty) 5. these (two million tourists—from number four) 6. this (Statue of Liberty), This (the story of how, when, and why the Statue came to the United States), these (how, when and why)

Exercise 5, p. 70: 1. this area = Delaware (or northeastern part of the United States) 2. these = the largest companies in the world 3. this state = Delaware; these companies = the largest companies, such as du Pont or the world's largest chemical companies 4. this accident = when the *Titanic* sank; that night = the night when the *Titanic* sank or the night of the accident 5. This news = the news that the *Titanic* sank or the news about the accident; this = the fact that *Titanic* could sink 6. this = eat fish 7. this previous advice = eating fish 8. this recent report = the report of a recent study (mentioned in number 7); This = people are eating fish instead of eating vegetables or exercising 9. this report = the recent report about eating fish and health; That = "Will people stop eating fish because of this report?"

Exercise 6, p. 72: 1. B 2. D 3. D 4. A

Exercise 7, p. 73: 1. B 2. A 3. A 4. A

Exercise 8, p. 73: 1. B 2. C

Exercise 9, p. 74: 1. delete "This bay is not very deep."; D 2. delete "Tuna salad sandwiches cost $1.75."; C

Exercise 10, p. 75: 1. C 2. A

Exercise 11, p. 76: 1. first A, fourth B, first C 2. second A, third B, fourth C 3. third A, first B, second C 4. fourth A, second B, third C

Exercise 12, p. 77:

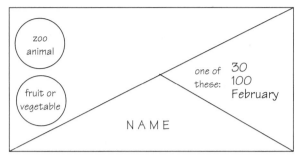

your teacher's name
[last: circle all the letters that are the same in
YOUR name and YOUR TEACHER'S name]

Exercise 14, p. 79: 1. B 2. A 3. A 4. B 5. B
Exercise 16, p. 81: 1. A 2. A 3. B 4. C 5. A
Exercise 18, p. 83: 1. A 2. B 3. A 4. A 5. B
Exercise 20, p. 85: 1. C 2. B 3. B 4. B 5. C
Exercise 22, p. 87: 1. A 2. A 3. A 4. C 5. A
Exercise 23, p. 88: 1. A 2. A 3. B 4. A 5. B 6. C
    7. C 8. B 9. C 10. A 11. B 12. A 13. A 14. B
    15. C 16. A 17. B 18. B 19. A 20. C 21. A
    22. A 23. C 24. B 25. A

Lesson 6

Exercise 1, p. 90:
Part 1: 1. $3.95 2. Extras 3. Diet Cola 4. Tuna Salad
    5. $4.00 6. $4.25 (because it's the Sandwich Set)
    7. 11 A.M. 8. because it's a sandwich shop 9.
    cheesecake or a dish of ice cream 10. $2.45 ($1.95
    plus 50¢ extra for cheese)
Part 2: 1. T 2. T 3. DK 4. T 5. F 6. F 7. T 8. DK
    9. F 10. T
Exercise 2, p. 91:
Part 1: Answers vary.
Part 2: 1. various answers 2. different 3. men who eat
    fish several times a week and men who eat fish
    only once a month 4. they are the same 5. prob-
    ably not; Japan and Greenland are listed because
    people in these countries eat a lot of fish. 6. be-
    cause it is very different from the information
    found in previous studies 7. the fact that people
    are eating fish instead of vegetables or instead of
    exercising 8. no; because he said this is not 100%
    true
Part 3: I.B. information II.A. Place II.B.1. several
    II.C. same III. surprising III.A. longer III.B. Ja-

pan IV. advice IV.B. vegetables, important V. Dr.
Katan's V.B. a lot of
Exercise 3, p. 95:
Part 1: Answers vary.
Part 2: Answers vary. (Possible morals: Don't be
    greedy. Don't lie.)
Part 3: Answers may vary. (Possible answers: 1. axe
    2. golden 3. ghost 4. take 5. axe 6. three 7. good
    8. ghost 9. about 10. want 11. threw 12. nothing)
Exercise 4, p. 99: Number three is true.
Exercise 5, p. 100: Answers vary.

Lesson 7

Task 1, p. 103:
Part 1:

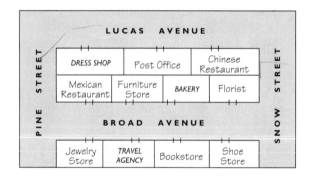

Part 2: 1. T 2. T 3. F 4. DK 5. F 6. T 7. T 8. T
    9. T 10. T
Task 2, p. 105:

Task 3, p. 107: 1. 16 2. $730 3. $7.10 4. 2 (Remem-
    ber that there are 6 people at the table, the five
    guests and Mrs. Hanks.) 5. C; 4 6. $90

Task 4, p. 108:

Part 1: A. 1. ie 2. ei 3. ei 4. ie 5. ie 6. ie 7. ie 8. ei
   B. 1. stopped 2. listened 3. offered 4. snowed
   5. played 6. enjoyed 7. asked 8. hoped 9. preferred 10. tried C. 1. cutting 2. beginning
   3. writing 4. controlling 5. meeting 6. learning
   7. flying 8. erasing D. 1. buys 2. cries 3. days
   4. flies 5. boys 6. cities

Part 4: Answers vary.

Task 5, p. 111:

Task 6, p. 112: 1. read, dead, dear, deer, deep 2. wood,
   good, gold, golf, wolf 3. cat, cut, cup, pup, pop
   4. card, care, fare, fame, game

Task 7, p. 114: 1. fall, ball, bell, belt, melt 2. call, ball,
   bald, bold, cold 3. mail, tail, tall, talk, walk 4. red,
   bed, bad, bat, rat

Task 8, p. 115: 1. boats, boots, books, looks, cooks
   2. wide, ride, rice, rise, rose 3. head, hear, bear,
   pear, wear 4. salt, sale, safe, cafe, cake

Task 9, p. 116: 1. red, bed, bad, sad, sat 2. tape, take,
   make, male, mile 3. ten, tan, man, map, mop
   4. went, west, best, belt, felt

Task 10, p. 117:

Lesson 8

Exercise 1, p. 119: various answers
Exercise 2, p. 122: various answers

Individual Vocabulary Notebook

Use these pages to make a list of new vocabulary words as you learn them in the text. Include the definition and an example. Continue the list in a notebook.

find out	find out = learn about. How did you find out about the accident?
1. SJUK	
2. HUGE	Size
3. develop	
4. Come up whit	Can you come up whit answer?
5. cut dow on	You cut dow on smoked.
6.	
7.	
8.	
9.	

10. _____ _____

_____

11. _____ _____

_____

12. _____ _____

_____

13. _____ _____

_____

14. _____ _____

_____

15. _____ _____

_____

16. _____ _____

_____

17. _____ _____

_____

18. _____ _____

_____

19. _____ _____

_____

20. _____ _____

_____

21. _____ _____

_____

22. _____ _____

_____

23. _____ _____

_____

24. _____ _____

_____

25. _____ _____

_____

26. _____ _____

_____

27. _____ _____

_____

28. _____ _____

_____

29. _____ _____

_____

30. _____ _____

_____

31. _____ _____

_____

32. _____ _____

_____

33. _____ _____

_____

34. _____ _____

_____

35. _____ _____

_____

36. _____   _____
                         _____

37. _____   _____
                         _____

38. _____   _____
                         _____

39. _____   _____
                         _____

40. _____   _____
                         _____

41. _____   _____
                         _____

42. _____   _____
                         _____

43. _____   _____
                         _____

44. _____   _____
                         _____

45. _____   _____
                         _____

46. _____   _____
                         _____

47. _____   _____
                         _____

48. _____   _____
                         _____

49. _____ _____
_____

50. _____ _____
_____

51. _____ _____
_____

52. _____ _____
_____

53. _____ _____
_____

54. _____ _____
_____

55. _____ _____
_____

56. _____ _____
_____

57. _____ _____
_____

58. _____ _____
_____

59. _____ _____
_____

60. _____ _____
_____

61. _____ _____
_____

62. _____ _____

63. _____ _____

64. _____ _____

65. _____ _____

66. _____ _____

67. _____ _____

68. _____ _____

69. _____ _____

70. _____ _____

71. _____ _____

72. _____ _____

73. _____ _____

74. _____ _____

75. _____ _____

76. _____ _____

77. _____ _____

78. _____ _____

79. _____ _____

80. _____ _____

81. _____ _____

82. _____ _____

83. _____ _____

84. _____ _____

85. _____ _____

86. _____ _____

87. _____ _____

88. _____   _____
    _____

89. _____   _____
    _____

90. _____   _____
    _____

91. _____   _____
    _____

92. _____   _____
    _____

93. _____   _____
    _____

94. _____   _____
    _____

95. _____   _____
    _____

96. _____   _____
    _____

97. _____   _____
    _____

98. _____   _____
    _____

99. _____   _____
    _____

100._____   _____
    _____